YOUR LEGACY

YOUR LEGACY

=== The Greatest Gift ===

DR. JAMES DOBSON

New York   Boston   Nashville

Unless otherwise noted, Scriptures are taken from the HOLY BIBLE: NEW INTERNATIONAL VERSION®. Copyright © 1973, 1978, 1984 by International Bible Society. Used by permission of Zondervan Publishing House. All rights reserved.

Scriptures noted ESV are taken from The Holy Bible, English Standard Version, copyright © 2001 by Crossway Bibles, a division of Good News Publishers. Used by permission. All rights reserved.

Scriptures noted KJV are taken from the King James Version of the Bible.

Scriptures noted NKJV are taken from the NEW KING JAMES VERSION. Copyright © 1979, 1980, 1982, Thomas Nelson, Inc., Publishers.

Scriptures noted NLT are from the *Holy Bible*, New Living Translation, copyright © 1996. Used by permission of Tyndale House Publishers, Inc., Wheaton, Illinois 60189. All rights reserved.

FaithWords
Hachette Book Group
237 Park Avenue
New York, NY 10017

www.faithwords.com

Printed in the United States of America

RRD-C

First Edition: September 2014
10 9 8 7 6 5 4 3 2 1

FaithWords is a division of Hachette Book Group, Inc.
The FaithWords name and logo are trademarks of Hachette Book Group, Inc.

The Hachette Speakers Bureau provides a wide range of authors for speaking events. To find out more, go to www.hachettespeakersbureau.com or call (866) 376-6591.

The publisher is not responsible for websites (or their content) that are not owned by the publisher.

Library of Congress Cataloging-in-Publication Data

Dobson, James C., 1936-
    Your legacy : the greatest gift / Dr. James Dobson. — First [edition].
        pages cm
    ISBN 978-1-4555-7343-1 (hardcover) — ISBN 978-1-4555-7627-2 (large print hardcover) — ISBN 978-1-4555-8779-7 (Spanish trade pbk.) — ISBN 978-1-4555-8778-0 (Spanish ebook) — ISBN 978-1-4789-2549-1 (audio download) — ISBN 978-1-4789-2548-4 (audiobook) — ISBN 978-1-4555-7342-4 (ebook) 1. Families—Religious aspects—Christianity. 2. Families—Religious life. 3. Legacies. I. Title.
    BT707.7D63 2014
    261.8'3585—dc23
                                                                    2014017849

This book is dedicated to my great-grandfather, George Washington McCluskey, whom I never met. Nevertheless, I will always be indebted to him. He is the great patriarch of our family who left us the legacy of a lifetime.

CONTENTS

PREFACE

Your Legacy is a book about building meaningful faith in children and passing it along to future generations. For parents who believe passionately in Jesus Christ and anticipate His promised gift of eternal life, there is no higher priority in life than providing effective spiritual training at home. Unless we are successful in introducing our children to Him, we will never see them again in the afterlife. Everything else is of lesser priority. But securing the baton of faith in the hands of our sons and daughters is often difficult in today's shockwave world. Indeed, there is an unrelenting tug-of-war occurring for their hearts and minds. Fortunately, we are not alone in this assignment. God loves our children even more than we do, and He is faithful to hear and answer our prayers.

I have written many books in the past forty years, but *Your Legacy* is, I believe, the most significant. It provides the punctuation for all that has gone before.

Dr. James Dobson

YOUR LEGACY

CHAPTER ONE

The First Generation

The year was 1862 and the Civil War was tearing our young nation apart. Abraham Lincoln was the newly elected president, and his Army of the Potomac was losing one battle after another to General Robert E. Lee's Confederate Army.[1] It was a troubled time for a country that had begun with such promise.

On November 15 of that year, a baby boy was born to the McCluskey family in Pine Bluff, Arkansas, and they named him George Washington in honor of the Father of our Country. Mr. and Mrs. McCluskey were devout Christians and their son was raised in the "fear and admonition of the Lord."

George grew up and married Alice Turnell on November 14, 1886. They lived happily together for forty-nine years. He died at seventy-two years of age. Alice lived to be ninety-eight. They were to become my great-grandparents. He was a farmer on the plains of Texas for many years until an itinerant minister came to their town. George went to hear him preach and had a dramatic encounter with Jesus Christ. In days to come, he felt a definite "call" to the ministry and spent the rest of his life working as an evangelist and a pastor for numerous churches. "Winning people to Christ" was his greatest passion. He was about six feet five inches tall, about the same height as Abraham Lincoln.

G. W. McCluskey died on November 14, 1935. His granddaughter became my mother, and she was two months pregnant with me when her grandpa died. I regret that I never had an opportunity to meet this good man. As you will soon understand, I owe him so much!

Alice, who I knew as Nanny, helped to raise me. One of my earliest memories was lying in a bassinet and looking up at the woman who smiled down upon me. She wore a knitted cap that had fuzzy balls dangling from yarn. Though it might be difficult to believe, I have vague memories of reaching up from my tiny crib and grasping the balls. I couldn't have been more than fifteen months old. That introduction to Nanny was one of my earliest glimmers of self-awareness, and from it came the beginnings of my love for my great-grandmother. An even earlier memory was of being held in someone's arms, perhaps it was Nanny, who was feeding me something that smelled like the baby food known then as Pabulum. I still recall how it tasted. (Not very good.)

In years that followed, Nanny talked often to me about her life with George. She never called him by his first name, of course. He was always referred to as "my husband," or "your great-grandfather." Nanny told me fascinating stories about their life in a cabin on the frontier and how "panthers" (mountain lions) would prowl around at night trying to kill their squealing pigs. My eyes must have been as big as saucers as the imagery of those big cats became real.

Nanny also told me about the prayer life of her husband. For the last several decades of his life, this patriarch of the family prayed specifically for the spiritual welfare of his children and for those yet to come. He devoted the hour from 11 a.m. to 12 noon every day for this purpose. Toward the end of his life, he said the Lord had made a very unusual promise to him. Reverend McCluskey had been assured that every member of four generations of his family would be Christians. We'll see how that prophecy manifested itself through the next eighty years and continues to this day.

What an incredible heritage has been handed down to our family. It is remarkable to think that a man in his seventies, whom I would not know until we get to heaven, was on his knees talking to God about his progeny. Now my great-grandfather's prayers reach across four generations of time and influence our lives today.

In 2012, my son and daughter, Ryan and Danae, went with me to find the McCluskey gravesite for the first time. We located it in Placid, Texas, an hour's drive from Austin. There are only thirty-two people living in Placid today, most of them elderly. There are no stores or businesses remaining in that place. An old brick schoolhouse still stands where children once learned, laughed, and played. It is decrepit and boarded up now. A small ramshackle general store has survived but is locked up tight. This is where people once bought groceries and played dominoes in the distant past. A rusted Conoco gasoline pump leans out front. We worked our way around to the other side of what used to be a town and found an abandoned cemetery. Eighteen members of the McCluskey family are buried there. Among them are the graves of my great-grandfather, George, and his wife, Alice (Nanny). His tombstone is inscribed with the words, "George W. McCluskey. He died as he lived—a Christian." What an understatement!

We knelt there at the gravesite and each of us prayed because it seemed like holy ground. Each of us thanked the Lord for the influence of these godly ancestors and for the prayers of my great-grandfather. As Danae was praying, a beautiful rainbow appeared above us. Tears flowed down her cheeks as she spoke from her heart. A caretaker told us it is rare to see such a breathtaking scene in that dry hill country. Ryan was the last to pray, and he thanked the Lord for the four generations of our family who have lived for Jesus Christ, each in their time. Ryan said that George McCluskey would have wanted to know that he and Danae are also serving Christ, and as such, are members of the fifth generation. Ryan and his wife, Laura, are teaching their two children to love Jesus, too. They will soon take their places as representatives of the sixth. How powerful are the prayers of a man whose petitions have reached his children, grandchildren, great-grandchildren, great-great-grandchildren, and great-great-great-grandchildren. We are all beneficiaries of his devotion.

Hebrews 12:1 tells us "we are surrounded by a great cloud of witnesses." I've always wondered who is in that cloud. Are they the patriarchs of the Bible or the other saints who have gone before, or perhaps angels who are looking down on us? I don't know. I'll leave it to the theologians to interpret for us. But I'd like to think the McCluskeys are watching from above. Regardless, there's one thing I know. We will see them again.

Have you thought about the legacy you want to leave to your children and generations to come? That is a question every Christian parent should consider. The implications of it are breathtaking. If the objective of living is to pass on a heritage of faith to those you love and to be with them throughout eternity, I suggest that you be intentional about preparing for it now.

That is what I want to share with you in the pages to follow.

CHAPTER TWO

The Second Generation

If you have ever watched track and field competitions, you know that relay races are usually won or lost in the transfer of the baton. A runner rarely drops the prize on the backside of the track. The critical moment occurs when he burns around the final turn and prepares to hand the baton to the next runner. If either of them has fumble-fingers and fails to complete a secure pass, their team usually loses.

So it is with the Christian life. When members of one generation are committed to the Gospel of Jesus Christ and are determined to finish strong, they rarely fumble the baton. But getting the handoff securely in the hands of children can be difficult and risky. That is when Christian commitments between generations can be dropped. It isn't always the fault of the parents. Some young runners refuse to reach out and grasp the baton. Either way, there is nothing more tragic than failing to transfer the baton to those who come after.

Let me tell you how the transmission of the Christian faith was handled between George and Alice McCluskey and their children. We recently discovered two yellowed biographies that I now treasure. The first describes my great-grandfather, and the second my grandfather, both on my mother's side. My daughter discovered these documents when she was searching through boxes of family memorabilia. They reveal some of the stories and factual information shared above. These statements were written by two contemporaries and typed on old typewriters, eighty and sixty-nine years ago. There were handwritten, eyewitness notations in the margins. What treasures they are!

The McCluskeys had two daughters who survived childhood. They were named Bessie and Allie. Bessie became my grandmother and Allie my great-aunt. They both gave their hearts to the Lord on the same night, and in time, each of them married preachers. I will tell you about their journeys in a moment. Bessie and Allie had five children between them, four girls and one boy. All four of the girls married preachers, and the boy became one. My great-grandfather's prayers were being answered year by year.

First, let me tell you the remarkable story of Michael Vance Dillingham who became my maternal grandfather. He was five feet two inches tall and his family would later call him "Little Daddy." That is the way I knew him. M.V. was something of a scoundrel in his early life. He was a hard drinker and a gambler. His biographer described him this way:

Sometime before the year 1900, in Comanche County, Texas, a group of God-fearing people united together to pray for the "lost" [unsaved] around them. Number one on that list was Michael Vance Dillingham [also called Mike or M.V.]. He was the instigator of community all night "shindigs," referring to card games, drinking and other worldly amusements of that day. They felt if somehow Dillingham became a Christian, others would follow him. However, Mike had not the slightest interest in his spiritual welfare. He was a carefree, fun loving widower in his thirties.[1]

After the death of his first wife, M.V. became embroiled in a bitter dispute with his former brother-in-law, probably over an unpaid gambling debt. His hatred for this man was so intense that he bought a gun and decided to kill him on sight. One night, M.V. took the gun and set out to murder his brother-in-law. As he walked down a dark road, he passed a revival service featuring the preaching of an anointed minister.

The Christians who had been praying for M.V. had sponsored a series of nightly meetings in their small Texas town. Their first challenge was to find a structure in which to worship. Together they built what was known as a "brush arbor." It was made of small saplings stuck upright in the ground, with branches laid over the top. Rough-hewn benches were constructed for seats, and a handmade altar was placed across the front. For music, women played hymns on squeaky pump organs and provided accompaniment for the singing and special music. Lanterns lit the arbor at night.

My grandfather stopped on the road outside the structure. He was amused by the spectacle and stood with other scoffers in the shadows. But the sermon and the music stirred something deep within his soul. He had never heard the gospel before.

Though he had no intention of going into the service, he was drawn toward it. M.V. walked to the entrance of the brush arbor and then continued down a sawdust aisle. He knelt at the altar and wept as he repented of his sins. The biographer said he lay "prone" in front of the altar as he begged God for forgiveness.

M.V. then took the gun out of his belt and placed it on the altar. He stood, faced the little gathering, and told everyone that he had been forgiven and was a child of God. He confessed his hatred for his brother-in-law, but said he had nothing but love for him in his heart. He would later say, "I could have laid down my life for him then and there."

Dillingham left the gun on the altar, never to be retrieved. Shortly thereafter, he accepted a call to preach and began to share the "good news" with anyone who would listen. In coming years, he testified, witnessed, and exhorted wherever he went. His transformation was complete. The Apostle Paul writes in 2 Corinthians 5:17, "Therefore if any man is in Christ, he is a new creature: old things are passed away; behold, they become new." My grandfather became this "new man" that night in a brush arbor.

Here's where the hand of the Lord intervened dramatically in our family. George McCluskey and his wife were many miles away, but they were also doing everything they could to bring people to Christ. George was still a farmer in San Saba County, Texas, but he decided to hold a revival meeting in the local town. He began by building…you guessed it…a brush arbor. Although he didn't know Michael Dillingham, George McCluskey had heard about the younger man's spiritual conversion. He wrote and invited him to come preach and sing at his revival meeting. M.V. accepted the request, and that was the first time my future great-grandfather met my future grandfather. They joined forces in a common cause and served Christ together for many years.

To top it off, M.V. fell in love with Bessie. She was George and Alice's oldest daughter, whom we would later call "Big Mama" for good reason. They were married after a five-year courtship. Thus, my bloodline was established. Imagine the consequences for my family if M.V. had shot his brother-in-law the night he gave his heart to the Lord.

M.V. and Bessie ("Little Daddy" and "Big Mama" to our family) set out together to serve the Lord, but they had no formal training or theological instruction. My grandfather knew he needed help. He once saw an ad offering information on how to preach for the price of one dollar. M.V. sent in the money and received this printed recommendation: "Have something to say, say it, and sit down." He said that was the best advice he ever received.

The Dillinghams had few of this world's resources or comforts. They went into communities to preach, often without invitations or places to stay, and certainly without promise of remuneration. When churches and schools were closed to them, they worshipped in homes, rented vacant buildings, or prayed in brush arbors. Their spirits were dauntless, although there were many times when they didn't know where their next meals would come from. When food was not available, they fasted and prayed.

At times, overripe fruit and rotten eggs were hurled at them from darkened shadows. It didn't discourage them. They held street meetings, sang songs, pumped squeaky organs, and strummed out-of-tune guitars in Texas, Oklahoma, Arkansas, and New Mexico. They traveled on dusty trains, on horseback, buggies, and bumpy wagons. But they also preached to great crowds with much success. As the years unfolded, they held ten pastorates from 1908 to 1944 when Reverend Dillingham died. Their churches grew rapidly and people responded to the simple truths of Scripture.

Frankly, I am embarrassed to admit how quickly some of us today complain about criticism and persecution for our Christian beliefs. We know little of the deprivations that our ancestors suffered. Most of them never wavered in their faith or their mission. This is the heritage handed down from my forbearers.

Fulfillment of "the promise" made to George McCluskey was right on schedule. So far, every member of two generations was not only a believer in Christ, but each of them was a preacher or was married to one. And there were still two generations to come.

CHAPTER THREE

The Third Generation

The Dillinghams had three daughters along the way. Another one died in infancy. The girls were "preacher's kids," which is not an easy way to grow up. My mother was second among them and she was a rather strong-willed child. She became even tougher as an adolescent and young adult. She had heard all the talk about her grandfather's prayers and she vowed she would never marry a minister.

A person should be very careful about telling God what he or she will not do. In time, my mother came to understand the foolishness of that statement.

That brings my father's story into the picture from the Dobson side of the family. When he was a baby, he was dedicated at an altar one night by a highly respected minister named Doctor Godby. He had preached that Sunday morning, and afterward, he remained on the platform all afternoon praying for the evening service. That night, Jimmy was brought to the altar and placed in Doctor Godby's arms. The old man anointed the baby's head with oil and prayed for him. Then the minister said, "This little boy will grow up to preach the Gospel of Jesus Christ all over the nation." There were no other ministers in the Dobson family. That prophetic word from Reverend Godby was shared with Jimmy when he was grown, but to my knowledge, not before.

When my father was six, he told his family that he wanted to be an artist. He was the only member of five Dobson children who knew from childhood what they wanted to do with their lives, but Jimmy was emphatic about his plans. Through elementary school and well into high school, he never wavered. He wanted to be a classical artist, in the manner of Michelangelo, Leonardo, Rafael, Rembrandt, and the other legendary painters and sculptors throughout history. Art was the passion of his life.

Jimmy was seventeen years old, walking to school one day, when out of nowhere the Lord spoke to him. He said, "I want you to preach the Gospel of Jesus Christ all over the world." It wasn't spoken in an audible voice, of course, but the young man knew he had been spoken to.

My dad was terrified. He said, "No, Lord! No! No! No! I have my life already planned. Talk to one of my four brothers. They don't know what they want to do in life. My course is set."

Jimmy tried to argue down what continued to be an irrepressible "call." He would get it all settled and tucked away, but it kept coming back even stronger than before. He couldn't shake it off. He told no one about his inner conflict except his godly mother, and she didn't believe it. I wonder if she recalled the prophetic words of Doctor Godby.

Jimmy's senior year in high school was a time of turmoil. As he approached graduation, his father came to him and said, "Pick out any college in the country you want to attend, and I'll send you there." Grandfather Dobson owned portions of five Coca-Cola plants among other enterprises, and he was very successful financially. Even though he made a lot of money, R. L. Dobson never gave up his job as a conductor on the Kansas City Southern Railroad.

My dad was the youngest of five brothers, and the other four had gone on to colleges or universities by the time Dad was in high school. One of them, Willis, later earned a Ph.D. in Shakespearian English from the University of Texas and was head of the English Department for a Christian college for forty years. He committed his life to Christ when he was nine years old and never veered from it until he died one Sunday morning at seventy-four. Toward the end of his life, Willis was a compassionate and godly man who was kind and gentle with everyone. He regularly served ice-cold bottles of Coca-Cola to the trash collectors on hot summer days. At seventy, he ran a shuttle service with his car, taking "old people" to and from church. He once gave his brand-new overcoat to a homeless person he met on the street. It was, he said, "because I had two coats. He had none." His son, who was there when the gift was made, cried when he told me about it.

Neither Willis nor his brothers knew the dilemma Jimmy was facing. Was he going to attend a seminary, as he knew God wanted, or enroll in a school to prepare him for a career in art? He had to decide, but the internal battle was intense. One morning he got out of bed and as his feet touched the floor, he seemed aware of the voice of the Lord again. It said, "Today, you will make your choice."

Jimmy went to school that morning in a state of depression. He could think about nothing else as he moved from class to class. After school, he walked home still in despair. What would he do?

He found the house empty that afternoon and began to pray about the decision. He was in the living room of what we all came to know as "the Big House." He paced back and forth, praying as he weighed his alternatives. Then suddenly, as he would later describe, he looked up to heaven and said aloud, "It is too great a price, and I won't pay it!" There was defiance in his voice. He said the Spirit of the Lord left him like one person walking away from another.

A few minutes later, my dad's mom came home. She was a ninety-seven-pound mother of six whom we would call "Little Mother." She found her youngest son pale and shaken. His hands were trembling.

"Honey, what's wrong?" she asked.

Jimmy tried to tell her about his struggle with a call to preach, but she brushed it off. She said, "Oh, you're just emotional. Let's pray about it." They knelt together and Little Mother began to pray for her son. She was a "prayer warrior," but this time the heavens were brass above her. About three minutes later she stopped in mid-sentence.

"I don't understand it," she said. "I can't pray for you. Something is wrong."

My dad replied, "You don't understand it, Mama, but I do. I have just said no to God, and He is gone."

There are numerous references in Scripture to men who were called by God for specific purposes, but they refused. Moses was one of the first. Jehovah spoke to him from a burning bush and ordered him to lead the Children of Israel out of slavery in Egypt. But Moses had the temerity to argue with the Holy One of Israel. He offered a lame excuse: "O Lord, I have never been eloquent, neither in the past nor since you have spoken to your servant. I am slow of speech and tongue" (Exod. 4:10).

Have you ever told God He was being unreasonable when He asked you to do something? I have and it is risky business. We read in Exodus:

Jehovah said sternly, "Who gave human beings their mouths? Who makes him deaf or mute? Who gives him sight or makes him blind? Is it not I, the Lord? Now go; I will help you speak and will teach you what to say." (Exod. 4:11–12)

Amazingly, Moses continued to object, saying, "O Lord, please send someone else." Then the Lord's anger burned against Moses (Exod. 4:13–14).

Other patriarchs of the Bible initially said "no" to the Almighty. Jacob wrestled all night with an angel from God.[1] Gideon refused to lead the armies of Israel against the Mideonites until finally yielding. With only 300 men, he won a stunning victory against 180,000 armed soldiers.[2] Jonah was unwilling to preach to the wicked people of Nineveh and tried to run away from God. He soon found himself in the belly of a "big fish" and had a change of mind.[3]

There have been millions of Christians in more recent times who have also argued with God. Dr. Jim Kennedy was one of them. He refused a call to preach because he wanted to be a dance instructor for the Arthur Miller dance studios. Imagine that! He ran from God for more than a year before yielding. Then he went to seminary and became a much-loved and respected pastor of Coral Ridge Presbyterian Church in Ft. Lauderdale, Florida. He also founded a witnessing program called Evangelism Explosion, through which more than six million people came to Christ. Kennedy almost missed the call of a lifetime.[4]

My dad was just as headstrong. He had his own way and enrolled in the prestigious Art Institute of Pittsburgh. He turned out to be a very talented young man. Jimmy Dobson graduated at the top of his class. On graduation morning, his paintings were sitting on easels across the platform, each bearing the designation "Number 1." As he was walking down the aisle to receive the honor, a verse of Scripture echoed back from his childhood: It said, "Except the Lord build the house, they labor in vain that build it" (Ps. 127:1 KJV).

Dad came back from Pittsburgh to his parents' home in Shreveport, Louisiana, in hot pursuit of a dream. However, the Great Depression had descended on the American economy and there were no jobs available. Jimmy not only couldn't find a position as an artist, he was unable to secure *any* kind of work. Weeks and months went by without success. Finally, he was hired by a small Texaco service station at the edge of town where cars seldom came. He was paid one dollar a day to pump gasoline, clean bathrooms, and remove grease off the pavement. My dad would refer to that time as his days of "Egyptian Bondage." The Lord left him in this dead-end job for seven years until he became sick of himself and his lofty dreams.

Then Jimmy met a pretty girl named Myrtle Georgia Dillingham. Some say she looked rather like the 1920s starlet Clara Bow. Meeting her was the only exciting thing going on in my dad's life and he was crazy about her. Unfortunately, she didn't feel the same way about him. He pursued her unsuccessfully for months. Finally, their relationship came to a crisis point one evening at her parents' home. He was trying to win her affections but she treated him rudely. My dad was a proud man, and he finally had enough. Jimmy looked deeply into her eyes for a moment without speaking. It was his way of saying, "Goodbye, my love." Then he walked out the door. She knew she had pushed him too far and he wasn't coming back. My future existence hung in the balance. Get it?

My dad was six feet four and he always walked fast. It was raining and Myrtle ran after him. She was barefoot and he heard the patter of her feet approaching him from behind. She caught up with him a block from her house. In that moment, as the rain soaked them both, she fell madly in love with James C. Dobson. She adored him for the rest of her life.

Jimmy and Myrtle wanted to get married but it was impossible to survive financially as a couple. My dad hardly earned enough money to feed himself, much less support a wife. They decided to wed secretly so that they could continue to live with their parents. It was three months before their families learned that they were husband and wife.

One night when my father was visiting his secret wife at her parents' home, my grandfather began to worry about what the couple was doing in the living room. He sneaked out the back door and crawled along a side fence where he could look through the window. He was shocked to see Jimmy and Myrtle kissing and hugging. He burst through the front door and accused my dad of taking liberties with his daughter. What a surprise it was for Little Daddy to discover that his darlin' daughter was married, and that the man who had been "taking liberties" was his son-in-law. M.V. would soon learn to love Jimmy Dobson like his own flesh and blood, but he and Bessie were pretty ticked at first. How could this Texaco employee take care of their daughter, especially when he couldn't even afford to rent an apartment?

Surprisingly, my dad had not told "Myrt" (his pet name for her) about his call to preach. That was a deep dark secret that he didn't want to even think about. He also knew she probably wouldn't have married him if she had known he might become a preacher, like the rest of the men in her family. As far as Myrtle knew, she was the wife of a "starving artist" who had plans for eventual greatness. They weren't going to church or living a committed Christian life. Among their church friends, they would have been called "backsliders."

About that time, a local church scheduled a revival meeting in Shreveport and called Rev. Bona Fleming as the evangelist. There was no television or Internet available in those days, and a revival in a growing, well-attended church caused quite a stir. The Dobson family was following the event with interest, too. The grown children decided to meet at their parents' home and go to the evening service together. When the time came to leave, four sons, their sister, and mother crammed into the family car. Then Willis noticed that Jimmy was not with them.

He said, "Hey, where's Jim? He's not in the car."

Willis climbed out and went looking for his youngest brother. He searched all over the house, calling his name. My dad was hiding on the side porch, sitting in a swing. Finally, Willis found him. He came and stood before Jimmy, who was looking down.

"Jim," he said, "aren't you going with us to the service tonight?"

"No, Willis," my dad said without looking up. "I'm not going tonight and I am *never* going again."

Willis, who had a great love for the Lord, said nothing. As my dad was still sitting with his head down, he saw big tears splashing on his brother's shoes.

My dad was touched and he said to himself, "If Willis cares this much about me, I will go because he wants me to."

Because Jimmy had made everyone late, the service had already started by the time all seven Dobsons filed in. The church was completely packed except for some seats on the front row. A young woman was singing as they walked down the aisle, and the lyrics resonated in my dad's heart. Suddenly, he yielded. The struggle was over. He said, "All right, Lord. I will do what You want. If You ask me to give up my dreams of being an artist and become a preacher, I will do it. I'm tired of running away. You can have me." He was weeping by the time he reached the front pew.

The singer finished and sat down. Reverend Fleming perceived that something significant had taken place in the young man sitting before him. He walked over to the edge of the platform, put his foot on the altar, and leaned forward. He then pointed directly at my dad and said,

"You, young man. Right there! Stand up!"

Jimmy stood obediently.

"Now I want you to tell all the people here tonight what the Lord did for you while the young lady was singing."

My dad turned and told the crowd, as best he could, about yielding his will to the Lord. It might be said that this was his first brief "sermon." For the rest of his life, he was committed heart and soul to Jesus Christ.

Then he went home to his tiny apartment and told his new wife that she had, indeed, married a preacher. To her credit, she also gave her heart to the Lord and stood beside her husband in ministry for the next forty-three years. I never heard her complain once about being a preacher's wife. A woman can make or break a man, and my mom built my dad's confidence and helped make him the great man he became.

Two surprising things occurred in the next few days. First, as soon as my dad yielded to the call to preach, the Lord gave him back his art. There was nothing sinful or dishonorable about using the talent God had given to him. The problem was that his plans didn't include God. The lesson he was learning is that Jesus Christ will not settle for second place in our lives. He will be Lord of all or not Lord *at* all. It's true for you and me, too. Jesus spoke of that obligation when he said, "Take up your cross daily, and follow me" (Luke 9:23 NLT).

When Jimmy Dobson became a minister, he used his artistic talent in his work. When he died, he was head of the art department at MidAmerica Nazarene College (now University), where a fine arts building there bears his name today.[5] In short, my father gave up nothing. It was all returned to him with a cherry on the top. Our home is decorated with his beautiful paintings, and his works hang in hundreds of homes, buildings, and churches. Nothing was wasted.

The other thing that happened is that the president of the Art Institute of Pittsburgh wrote my father a letter offering him a prime teaching position at a fabulous salary. It was precisely the kind of job he had been searching for while languishing at the Texaco station. However, that letter became lost on the president's desk and wasn't found until months later. The president then sent the original letter to my dad, along with a cover letter describing his mistake. He wrote, "I wondered why you didn't even do me the courtesy of responding to my offer."

If my dad had received the original letter when it was written, he would have jumped all the way to Pittsburgh. However, by the time the second letter arrived, my dad had accepted the call to preach and the issue of his career was settled forever.

Little Mother, my dad's mom, had never stopped praying for her son during his time of travail. Clearly, God was intervening in his life even when there was no evidence of His presence. We see again in this account the power of prayer in the lives of His people.

The story didn't end there, of course. In fact, there were huge obstacles in the road ahead. Jimmy was a very shy young man with the temperament of an artist. He had never spoken a word publicly in his life except for that night at the service. He had not made so much as an announcement in church. Humanly speaking, he was wholly unsuited for a career in the ministry and he knew absolutely nothing about that field. Also, he had missed his opportunity to go to seminary. Even his family thought he was making a huge mistake, although they only muttered their misgivings among themselves.

My dad asked the Lord, "What am I going to do now?" Then he heard a compassionate voice that said reassuringly, "I'll give you a little help."

My father threw himself into the challenge. In the first week after his decision, he gave up his job as (by then) manager of the Texaco service station and began working on a local preacher's license. He finished a home study course in record time, working ten to twelve hours a day through the scorching summer months. He preached a few times at the invitation of his in-laws, the Dillinghams, and began to get the hang of it. But he was still very green.

He then contacted the presiding elder in his denomination and asked if he could preach occasionally in his district. The elder reluctantly referred him to one of the churches he

supervised. It was located some distance away in Mena, Arkansas, where the local congregation was looking for a pastor. They
invited Jimmy to come preach what was known as a "trial sermon." It was the first and only time he would submit himself to
that indignity. At that point, however, he was hardly in a favor-
able bargaining position.

Jimmy and Myrtle prayed in the car on the way to the train
depot and asked for God's blessing the next morning. Myrtle
kissed him warmly, and when he looked at her, she had tears
in her eyes. Having been brought up in a minister's home, she
knew far better than her husband about the trials and sacrifices
that a pastor and his family would endure, especially in a small
church. As he boarded the train, she said again, "You can be
sure I'll be praying for you."

The journey took almost a full day, and Jimmy spent that
entire time going over his two sermons meticulously. When he
arrived in Mena, he checked into his hotel and then walked
around the town and past the church. Then he returned to his
room and tried to sleep. After a fitful night, Sunday morning
came creeping in. Dad was nervous as a cat.

Years later, he wrote about the events of that day, which tells
us quite a bit about the character and humility of the man.

I took my Bible and walked again toward the church. When
I was about a block away, I saw another man who looked
strikingly like a preacher with a Bible under his arm. He
was approaching the church from the other direction. We
met on the front steps and I introduced myself.

"Hi, I'm James Dobson." I said. "My presiding elder,
Brother Brian, sent me to preach two trial sermons at this
church today."

The man looked surprised and said, "There must be some mistake. I am Ben Harley, and Brother Brian told me distinctly to come here and preach two trial sermons today."

I was utterly dismayed and confused by his statement. What was the ethical thing to do in a case like that? Brother Harley was an older man with many years of experience. At length, I did the only thing there was to be done, which was to bow out gracefully.

"Since there was a mistake," I said, "you go ahead and preach and I will simply sit back and enjoy the services." (... what I was thinking about the presiding elder shouldn't be put in writing.)

Brother Harley would not hear of my suggestion. He proposed a better solution.

"Why not let me take one service and you take the other."

On his insistence, I agreed. I knew the odds were all against me. Brother Harley was already in a pastorate not many miles away and he wanted a change. I was looking for my first charge. He had 25 years of experience while I was a rank beginner. Nevertheless, I swallowed my pride and went through with it. Harley would preach the morning sermon and I would speak at night.

Harley's message was filled with clichés and bombast. He was preaching one of his favorite "sugar sticks" he had given before, and the audience was very receptive to him.

The evening service came quickly and it was my turn. I know the reader will forgive my candor when I reveal my miserable efforts to preach that night. I had no sugar sticks to offer. I became rattled and lost my confidence.

Ministers call that "getting in the brush." It was one of my most difficult experiences.

The board met immediately after the evening service and it took them only a few minutes to make their decision. The spokesman came to me first. He was "so sorry" to tell me that the church had called the other man. He said there was nothing against me, I was given to understand. He said I was a fine young man and he was sure I would find a good church somewhere, etc. He then gave me an envelope that he said contained some "expense money." He regretted that I had come so far. I thanked him and shook hands with Brother Harley and hoped that he would have a great ministry in Mena. Then I said "good-bye" and left.

When I got to the hotel, I opened the envelope that had been handed to me by the spokesman. It contained $3, which was considerably less than it had cost me to be there. I brushed a few tears from my eyes as I packed my suitcase to catch the night train back to Shreveport.

I was sitting there on the train thinking it all over, when a poor woman came down the aisle. She was dressed in cheap ragged clothes, and trying to handle several small children. They took the seat opposite me. Presently I heard the conductor come by and ask for her ticket. She began to cry. She had no ticket, she said, but she was going to see her mother who was at death's door. Her mother lived only a few miles down the track.

"Please don't put us off the train," she pleaded. "I promise to pay the railroad back when I get some money."

Before the conductor could reply, I took the three dollars out of my pocket and paid the woman's fare. I felt a great oneness with all the little people in the world that night.

It was not easy to tell Myrtle of my misfortunes, but once I began to recover, we laughed at the humor of my situation. My wife was understanding and supportive, as she has always been.

Those were the beginnings of darker days to come, but then we began to pray in earnest about how I could fulfill God's calling.

My dad was still trying to answer the "how to" question when he approached the presiding elder again. (Yes, it was *Brother Brian*.) Jimmy asked him if there was a little church somewhere—*anywhere*—that was in desperate need of a pastor. He specifically requested something small that he couldn't ruin. Dad would later wish he hadn't been so humble about his request because he got what he asked for.

Jimmy received an invitation several months later to serve as the pastor of a very small Nazarene Church in Sulphur Springs, a little farming community in East Texas. He was twenty-seven years of age. The church had only ten members, and the salary was whatever people put in the offering plate the previous Sunday. It was sometimes 50 cents or less. The ravages of the Great Depression were still very evident in rural Texas and no one had any money to spare. The farms had not been wired for electricity.

My paternal grandfather, R. L. Dobson, then died and willed Coca-Cola stock to his grown children, including my father. My family survived on the dividends. Without that money we might have starved, although God was working in our lives. Dad gave the balance of the money to the church every month to keep its doors open, and God blessed his ministry there. My parents were loved and the church grew rapidly. By the time they left four years later to accept other responsibilities, there were 250 members at Sulphur Springs Church of the Nazarene. They had built a parsonage and constructed a building for Christian education. Most important, Reverend Dobson had learned how to lead a flock.

My father went on to have a highly successful ministry as a pastor and evangelist. He led tens of thousands of people to Christ and became a very effective preacher. Even now, more than thirty years after his death, I hear often from older people who knew him and attended his services. Just recently, I received an unsolicited note from a man I've never met. This is what he wrote:

> When I hear you talk or read what you've written about your dad, it always takes me back some 50 years. A superintendent of our denomination told me that your father was the greatest evangelist in the church. This man emphasized how he affected entire congregations, including children.
>
> Keep following in your father's footsteps.

It was true. My father had a divine anointing and I was one of his converts. I'll tell you about that in the next chapter.

CHAPTER FOUR

The Fourth Generation

When my parents were still living in Shreveport in 1935, they began talking together about having a baby. Mom made an appointment with a family physician, Doctor Rigby, and after the examination he gave her discouraging news. He told her that because of her bone structure, she shouldn't try to become a mother. He warned her she could die in delivery.

It was a bitter pill to swallow, but my mother and father accepted the advice of Doctor Rigby. Months later, however, Dad told her he had been in prayer about their inability to have a child, and that the Lord had assured him they *would* have a baby...a son. I still have her written description of that conversation with my dad. She recalled, "I learned that when Jimmy said the Lord had spoken to him, he turned out to be right."

If my dad's words appear naïve and presumptuous today, you have to know something about his prayer life. Because he knew he was unprepared for the ministry, he prayed continually. It would be a lifelong pattern. On some days, he spent three to five hours alone with God. Dad was known in Sulphur Springs as the man with no leather on the toes of his shoes. He spent so much time on his knees that he wore out the toes before the soles. The Lord honored him and led him through his challenges and trials.

My mother soon became pregnant and I was delivered by Caesarian section on April 21, 1936. She suffered no complications and I was very healthy. Nevertheless, C-sections were dangerous procedures then and penicillin to prevent infections hadn't been invented. My mother was warned again by Doctor Rigby not to have another baby. His advice was even more emphatic than it had been the first time. Today C-sections are done by lateral incisions to avoid weakening the uterus. When I was delivered, however, the incision was made vertically, and subsequent deliveries could be fatal. This is why I was an only child.

Some people think "only children" are likely to be spoiled. To them I say, "Look at how great I turned out." (I hope you can see me smiling.) My mother and father loved me dearly. She had a remarkable knowledge of children and their care. She never took a class or read a book about mothering, but she had an intuitive understanding of the job. She also had a good support team around her, and she was a fast learner. In those days, the fundamentals of child rearing were taught to new moms by their mothers, grandmothers, aunts, friends, neighbors, and church ladies. In today's world, however, families are often separated geographically, and even if they live nearby, women are likely to be employed outside the home. They just don't have the time to advise the newcomers. Full-time moms are busy, too. They provide daily taxi service for their kids and struggle to maintain harried households. New moms are typically on their own.

Many years later I dedicated my first book for parents to my mother because she had earned it. It was called *Dare to Discipline* and incorporated many of the concepts and techniques I learned at her knee. Myrtle Dobson was a very bright and compassionate lady. My father and I also had a wonderful relationship. Indeed, I was a fortunate little boy.

We lived in a very small apartment that had only one bedroom, and my crib was positioned near my parents' bed. There was no other place to put it. My dad told me later that when I was two years old, it was not unusual for him to be wakened in the middle of the night by a small voice spoken just above a whisper,

"Daddy. Daddy."

He would answer, "What, Jimmy?"

I would then say, "Hold my hand."

My dad would sweep the darkness in search of my little hand, and the moment he engulfed it in his own, my arm would become limp and my breathing deep and rhythmical. I had gone back to sleep. I only wanted to know that he was there. He was always there for me until the day of his death.

I was raised in the church, and what I learned there was deeply ingrained in my mind. I grew up in a devout home where I learned to pray before I learned to talk. That was because I imitated the sounds of my parents' prayers before I knew the meaning of their words.

One Sunday night when I was four years of age, I was sitting by my mother at the back of the church on the right side. I remember the events of that evening as though they happened yesterday. Dad preached the sermon and then asked if there were people in the congregation who would like to come forward and give their hearts to the Lord. Many of them immediately began stepping into the aisle and going to the altar to pray. Without asking my mother, I joined them and knelt on the right side of the church. I remember crying and asking Jesus to forgive me and make me His child. Then I felt a big hand on my shoulder. My father had come down from the platform and knelt beside me to pray. My mother was also praying behind me. I wept like the baby I was.

Don't tell me that a small child is incapable of giving himself or herself to Christ. I know better. What I did on that night was not coerced or manipulated. It was my choice and I remember feeling so clean. After the service, my parents went to visit some members and left me in the car. I sat there thinking about what I had done and wondering about the meaning of it all. It had been a dramatic experience and I wanted to understand it. What occurred that evening turned out to be the highlight of my life. I sometimes say with a smile that everything since then has been downhill. It's a scary thing to experience the most significant moments of your life when you are four years of age.

I haven't lived a perfect life and am endowed by a generous assortment of flaws, but I have tried to please the Lord from that time to this. My experience at the altar had a profound impact on me. The boxes of memorabilia that I mentioned earlier contained a note written by my mother shortly after I had asked Jesus for forgiveness. She said I was very serious about it. A few weeks later, I fell and hurt my hand badly. I wailed, prompting my mother to suggest, "Why don't you pray and ask Jesus to take away the pain." I did, but then continued to cry.

Mom said, "Well, what did Jesus tell you?"

I said, "He told me He was busy watering the flowers and trees, but He would help me when he had time."

It made sense to me. My theology was a little confused, but the basic idea was right. I have called on the Lord many times since, often in utter desperation. On some occasions my prayers were answered the way I wanted. At other times He seemed to say, "Not now," or "No," or simply "Wait." This third reply is the most difficult to accept.

Back to our theme: H. B. London and I are first cousins (our mothers were sisters) and we were the first members of the fourth generation to reach young adulthood since "the promise" was given to our great-grandfather. We were both "only children" and grew up like brothers. We were roommates in college and during the first semester of our sophomore year, he announced that God had called him to be a minister. The news made me nervous because I realized I was the first member of four generations of my family who hadn't felt led into the ministry.

H.B. was ordained after graduating from seminary and served as a pastor for thirty-two years. He was also a "pastor to pastors" at *Focus on the Family* for twenty more, and spoke in more than one hundred denominations. He is semi-retired now and is finishing up his career again as an associate pastor and speaker.

I was marching to a different drum. I never heard the call that all of my relatives on my mother's side of the family experienced. After finishing college, I was accepted into graduate school at the University of Southern California. Seven years later, I finished a Ph.D. in child development and research design, and was offered a position on the medical staff of Children's Hospital of Los Angeles. I served there in the divisions of child development and medical genetics for seventeen years. For fourteen of those years, I was also a professor of pediatrics at USC School of Medicine. Those assignments prepared me for what was to come.

As much as I enjoyed academia, I became increasingly concerned about the institution of the family, which was starting to unravel. In fact, that was on my mind when I was in college. I was on my way to a tennis tournament one day when I was in my third year. The wife of one of my team members was in the car and she recalls how I spoke that day about the weakness of the American family, and said we needed to do what we could to strengthen it. I was twenty-one years old and the path I would take thereafter was beginning to come together. The year was 1957.

The culture was to deteriorate dramatically in the next decade. The social upheaval of the 1960s wreaked havoc on traditional values and was aimed squarely at the institution of the family. Without sounding like a self-appointed prophet, I saw clearly then and in the early seventies where the nation was headed. I anticipated the collapse of marriage, the murder of millions of preborn babies, and the abandonment of biblical morals. As always, my father had the greatest influence on my values and beliefs during this cultural revolution.

In graduate school during the late 1960s, the academic world began moving toward the legalization of abortion. Some of my professors were emphatic about it and they served to confuse me. I didn't understand the full implications of the issue, but I was irritated by the racist tone of these teachers. It is difficult to believe today what some of them actually said. One of them spoke for the others: "You know, so many inner-city children [meaning blacks] are being raised in squalid circumstances.

Most of them don't have fathers, and their mothers are often on drugs. These kids are growing up on the streets in violent gangs and have no adult supervision." (Here comes the punch line.) "Frankly, it would be better if these babies were not allowed to be born." I know now that they were reflecting the racist views of Margaret Sanger, founder of Planned Parenthood.

After hearing these comments the first time, I repeated them during dinner to my parents that evening. I remember so vividly my father being alarmed and angered by what the professors had said. He came off his chair and said, "Don't believe it, Jim. Please don't believe it for a moment. It is wrong and it is evil." Big tears welled in his eyes and streamed down his face when he said, "I will *never* cast a single vote for any politician who would kill one innocent baby." That phrase stayed with me and I have repeated it many times since.[1]

On this occasion and on many others, Dad was a beacon for me—a moral compass—that influenced my early professional life and steered me toward the principles of righteousness. Who knows how my value system would have evolved without this godly father who guided me into my adult years.

Those were also years of dramatic change for me. I met Shirley, who became my college sweetheart. We dated for three years before marrying on August 27, 1960. Shirley wanted to finish college and I was determined to be well into graduate school before taking on the responsibility of a wife and family. Noted Christian psychologist Dr. Clyde Narramore had advised me not to marry too quickly if I intended to get a Ph.D., which he strongly recommended I pursue. Five years passed before our daughter, Danae, came along. By then, I was only two years from completing my degree.

When I graduated in 1967, we began trying unsuccessfully to

conceive another child. Shirley underwent treatment for infertility, but it also failed. It was a time of constant disappointment, but at least we had one child. Couples that have "empty arms" hear bad news month after month. Their travail is like the agonizing death of a dream. My heart goes out to them.

Finally, Shirley and I decided to adopt a baby. We applied at a Christian agency, and four months later we received a call from a social worker saying, "Your baby is here."

We learned that a seventeen-year-old girl whom we have never met became pregnant out of wedlock, and she decided to carry the child to term. She allowed her baby to be adopted, and we were chosen by the agency to have that privilege. A beautiful little boy was handed gently to Shirley. The prayers of many years were answered on that day! We will be eternally grateful to the wonderful biological mother, whoever she is, that experienced the discomfort of pregnancy and the pain of childbirth in order to give life to our son, Ryan. Would you understand if I told you I have tears in my eyes as I write?

I grasped the full measure of my father's passion about the sanctity of human life and began trying to tell others about it. Babies are not "a blob of tissue" or "meaningless protoplasm," or "the products of conception," as the proponents of abortion told the American people. It was an insidious lie! Babies are creations of God who have eternal souls. I will be their advocate for the rest of my life.

Three years after Ryan was born, I was driving home from USC and listening to the radio. It was January 22, 1973, and a reporter announced, as best I recall, "The U.S. Supreme Court just issued a ruling on a case called *Roe* v. *Wade*.[2] [3] It legalized abortion on demand for any reason or no reason throughout nine months of pregnancy." I was deeply disturbed because I knew it would result in millions of tiny lives being lost. Even more dismaying was the lack of response from some of my Christian friends. My pastor, who I loved, didn't even mention the tragedy the next Sunday morning, nor did many other ministers and educators. Perhaps they agreed with my professor who said, "You know, it would be better…"

In thinking about that era now, I remember seeing a newsreel of President Franklin Delano Roosevelt's historic speech to Congress made the day after the bombing of Pearl Harbor, when he said, "December 7th, 1941, a date that will live in infamy…"[4] Though President Richard Nixon gave no speeches the day after January 22, 1973, it was also a date that will live in infamy. As I write today, almost 60 million babies have been put to death because of the decision made by seven imperious Justices. They are also dead now, and we should remember their names "in infamy." They are Justices Burger, Powell, Brennan, Marshall, Douglas, Stewart, and Blackmun. Only Justices White and Rehnquist dissented. The hands of the others are stained with the blood of millions of babies.[5]

Many of my Protestant brothers and sisters continued to miss the significance of the *Roe* v. *Wade* ruling. I'm not a Catholic, but I am grateful that their hierarchy *did* "get it." They spoke up fervently for life almost from the beginning. Even to this day, the Catholic community continues to carry the banner for unborn life. I am pleased to say that Protestants now appear to be awakening to the cause. Together, we are winning the battle for the hearts and minds of the American people. Nevertheless, a million babies die every year from "abortion on demand." *Life News* recently reported that 1.7 billion babies have been aborted worldwide since 1973.[6]

I spoke at the March for Life event on the National Mall in

Washington, D.C., on the forty-first anniversary of *Roe* v. *Wade*, January 22, 2014.[7] It was one of the coldest days of the year, as an icy wind swept the city. I was introduced by my son, Ryan, who is also a passionate defender of life. Then I walked to the podium and said a few words before offering the closing prayer. I was so cold on that below-zero day that my mouth hardly worked. As I looked out on that frozen crowd of sixty thousand people, I was gratified to see that most of the marchers were teens and young adults. They were applauding and cheering wildly for the Sanctity of Human Life. There is hope for America's future!

My purpose in sharing this brief history is not to boast but to show the linkage between my life's work and the early prophecy of my great-grandfather. Though I am not a minister, my ultimate objective has been to introduce people to Jesus Christ and to do it through the institution of the family. When I consider the call to preach responded to by every other member of my family, from my great-grandfather to H. B. London, I am inclined to wonder, "What's the difference in my case?" I rather think there is none.

And by the way, our son Ryan is an ordained minister in the Southern Baptist denomination and our daughter Danae is a speaker and writer in the service of Jesus Christ. They represent the fifth generation, and George Washington McCluskey must be smiling at us from heaven.

CHAPTER FIVE

What It All Means

The history I have shared with you to this point represents more than the biography of an American family from the late 1800s to our present day. If that's all there is, why bother? No, the significance of this account is centered on how "the faith of our fathers and mothers" was preserved and handed down to the present generation. Theirs was a remarkable achievement when you think about it. The message of the gospel survived among my forebears for more than one hundred years, despite an endless array of obstacles and challenges. They were not superhuman beings who escaped struggles and hardships. Life was no easier for them than for you and me. The McCluskeys and the Dillinghams, for example, dealt with the horrors of World War I in 1917–1918, the Spanish Flu that killed between 50 and 100 million people in 1919,[1] the Great Depression that ravaged the economy in 1929, and the Dust Bowl that drove

farmers from their land in the 1930s.[2] The Dillinghams also lost
a precious baby in the early 1900s.

My parents had their share of heartaches, too. My mother
loved Jimmy Dobson more than life itself until his sudden death
at sixty-six years of age. One Sunday afternoon on December
4, 1977, they were celebrating his sister's birthday. Dad held a
new baby and prayed a final prayer. Then they ate dinner, and
moments later, he leaned into the arms of my mom. He fell
on the floor and never breathed again. My cousin began CPR
immediately, but Dad was gone. Five minutes later, after no
other sign of life, he smiled broadly. I wish I knew who was there
to greet him. I will ask him about it when we meet in heaven.

My mom struggled mightily thereafter. From the time of
Dad's death, Myrtle Georgia Dillingham gave up on life. She
never recovered from the loss of the lanky "artist" she had
fallen in love with on a rainy night in Shreveport. She lived
eleven years longer than he, but died of a broken heart. She
literally grieved herself to death.

Time and space do not permit me to tell the entire story of
the intervening years, except to say that the love affair between
my parents had continued uninterrupted for more than four
decades. But all too quickly, it was over. I found my mother's
diary some years later and read an entry written on the first
anniversary of her husband's death. She penned:

> My precious darling. One year ago today you spent your
> last day on this earth. One year ago we spent our last night
> together. I have recalled our concluding activities through-
> out this day. You wanted to go to the shopping center to
> take your daily walk, although I thought you really wanted
> to look at the fishing rods. We window-shopped for a while,

and then you said, "Myrtle, you have to let go of me. Let me be free to go in and out of stores by myself…just to wander about free and alone."

I took your arm and said, "Go where you want, but let me go with you. Just let me walk beside you."

You shrugged and allowed me to tag along for a while. For nearly three months I had been with you constantly. I seemed to know that you were to be taken from me suddenly, and I wanted to be there—perchance I could do something to keep you alive. But a few minutes later you said, "Look down this long mall. You can see to its end. I want to walk down there and back again."

With that, I relented. But wouldn't you know, you took an escalator to one of the upper floors of the mall, removing you from my line of sight. I went looking for you frantically, and finally found you coming toward me with a grin on your face. You took me to a furniture store on the third floor and showed me a new chair that you had selected for my Christmas gift. It was your last day. Your last big fling.

On Sunday, December 4, you dressed early and then went downstairs to sit in your chair. I spent the morning upstairs. I wonder what you did those two hours. I know you read your Bible…what else? If I'd come down, you would have talked to me about it. Later we went to Elizabeth's house [Dad's sister, who lived in Kansas City]. You looked so handsome in your sports coat and beige slacks. I sat saying nothing, just watching you manipulate your long arms, legs and body. You held the baby…not too gracefully…since it was never easy for you to hold an infant. At the table, you sat by me and told a funny story about us. You prayed, and then gently, quietly, leaned toward me. Then your head and arm touched the table. They laid you on the floor. Bud breathed for you. He said you smiled once...your only sign of life. What did you see? Where did you go? My only comfort is that your last act on this earth was to lean toward me. Then you slipped away.

Very quickly I realized that you didn't exist anymore. Your name was removed from the church register. The bank took your name off our checks. Our home address was rewritten to include only my name. Your driver's license was invalidated. You were no more. Then I recognized that my name had changed, too. I had been proud to be Mrs. James C. Dobson, Sr. Now I was simply, Myrtle Dobson. I was not "we" any longer. I became me or I. And I am alone. You were my high priest. Inside, I'm broken, sad, stunned, alone. My house has lost its soul. You are not here!

People have told me the first year was the hardest. It's been one year and three days since you died, and tonight I am frantic with longing for you. Oh, dear God! It's more than I can bear. The sobs make my heart skip beats. I cannot see the paper. My head throbs. The house is lonely and still. Visions of you have been as real as if you were here and had not left me. Today, I thanked God for letting an angel watch over me. But how desperately I miss you!

I moved into the smaller bedroom today. I wish you were here to share that room with me. There are precious memories there. When I was ill four years ago, you prayed for me in that bedroom during the midnight hours. You lay on the floor, agonizing in prayer for me. We both knew the Spirit was praying through you. Later, the Lord led us to a doctor who helped me find my way back to health. Oh, how I loved you. I love your memory today.

There was another source of grief in the Dobson house. My dad had rescued a pitiful little dog, sort of a toy terrier, from a filthy pet shop three years before he died. His name was Benji, and he was barely alive when Dad found him. It took a year to get him healthy and by then, he had learned to worship my dad. Benji would sit on his lap hour after hour while his master read an endless array of sophisticated books. Dad and the pup were inseparable.

Benji watched my parents leave in the car on that ill-fated Sunday, but only one of them came back later that day. Benji had no way of knowing why the man he loved didn't return, and he was perplexed by it. He would stand with his ears erect at the top of the stairs leading down to the garage, waiting for my dad to drive in. He stood there for months hoping against hope.

Eighteen months later I came to Mom's home in Olathe, Kansas, to help close my dad's affairs and move Mother close to us. I put several suitcases on the bed and was packing Dad's clothes and belongings. Benji jumped up on the bed. He walked stiff-legged over to the suitcases and, cautiously and reverently, stepped into one of them. He smelled the clothes, one garment at a time, and then curled up on my dad's coat.

I said, "I know, Benji. I miss him, too."

Five years after my father's death, my mother contracted Parkinson's disease, and before long she was unable to speak or even recognize Shirley or me. She remained in a fetal position for years. Then one Sunday afternoon, I went to the nursing home to make sure she was being cared for properly. I walked into her room and, unbelievably, found her sitting upright in her bed. She was entirely lucid. I was shocked and sat on the side of her bed. I cradled her hands and told her how much all of us loved her. We talked about my dad and their love for each other. Then she looked into my eyes intently and said, "You know,

I've been thinking." How strange it was for a woman to say she had been thinking, when she had been completely incoherent for years. Then she revealed what was going through her mind, at least in the hours before I came.

She said with feeling, "I almost have it done."

"What do you mean, Mom?" I asked.

She repeated the words, "I almost have it done."

I realized she was talking about her physical struggle and her awareness that death was imminent. She would soon leave this life to go see my father. I thanked her for being such a great wife and mother, and we chatted together like in days gone by. Then I kissed her and said good-bye.

It was to be our final conversation on this earth. When I came to visit her a few days later, she was not lucid. Her momentary "recovery" was never repeated. Though my mom lived several more months, she never recognized me again. I believe the Lord gave me that final opportunity on a Sunday afternoon to tell my good mother that I loved her. She slipped away on a subsequent Sunday, and entered the presence of her Lord.

There are other stories behind the life and death of my relatives, which I won't share with you, except to say every member of my family went through similar trials. They encountered frustrations, rejection, disappointment, discouragement, failure, unanswered "whys," hypocrisy and apostasy in the church, and finally, sickness and death. If given a foothold, Satan would have used these and other trials to weaken their faith and destroy their testimony. But with God's help, they clung tenaciously to what they knew was right. There was no incident of infidelity, abuse, or divorce. Not one of them smoked or drank a drop of alcohol. Their lives were clean and upright. They had reached for a standard of holiness. But life isn't easy, even for saints.

I'm reminded of a beloved hymn, "Amazing Grace," which described the difficulties that characterized their journey. One verse says, "Through many dangers, toils, and snares, I have already come; 'twas grace that brought me safe this far, and grace will lead me home."[3] I praise the Lord for the "grace" that sustained three generations of my family and now four. I would not be writing to you today if they had given up when the pressure was on. That's why they are my heroes. To paraphrase the Apostle Paul in 2 Timothy 4:7, "[they] fought the good fight, finished the race, and kept the faith." And, I might add, they passed on their faith to the rest of us.

This is the "legacy" referred to in the title and content of this book. I have written dozens of books in the past forty years, but this one is the capstone. All the others have pointed, either indirectly or by implication, to this "passing on" of the Christian faith to one's children first, and then to preserving it for future generations. For this reason, I have quoted some of my previous works occasionally in this book. *Your Legacy* is a compendium of my thoughts about winning your children—and others—to Jesus Christ, because nothing comes close to it in significance.

Do you and I believe that? If so, then we should live every day with that objective in mind.

When I read the Bible today, I am aware that scribes and monks in the Dark Ages labored in monasteries or dreary caves and invested their lives in the tedious task of copying and preserving those priceless texts. What a gift they handed down to us. Now that treasure is in our hands. One of the most important questions Christians should ask is, how committed are we to the safeguarding of the faith for our progeny and for others they will influence. Those truths could be lost in a single generation. Will we hand down the "pearl of great price" to future generations?

That thought is addressed musically in the lyrics to the song "Find Us Faithful," written by Jon Mohr and sung by Steve Green.

Oh may all who come behind us find us faithful
May the fire of our devotion light their way
May the footprints that we leave
Lead them to believe
And the lives we live inspire them to obey

Oh may all who come behind us find us faithful

After all our hopes and dreams have come and gone
And our children sift through all we've left behind
May the clues that they discover and the memories they uncover
Become the light that leads them to the road we each must find

Oh may all who come behind us find us faithful[4]

What inspirational words are expressed in these lyrics! Let me say it again for emphasis: Staying faithful to our beliefs should be our ultimate priority. It has meaning not only for you and me but also for those who are yet to be born. That was the essence of my great-grandfather's daily prayer as he pleaded with God for the spiritual welfare of his family. Are you also praying for those in your bloodline? If you walk away from the truth, the linkage to the gospel may be severed for your descendents. Is there anything in life that is more important than that?

Let's talk more about it.

CHAPTER SIX

My Journey

It took me a while to get my own priorities straightened out. Indeed, I almost made the greatest mistake of my life in the early days of adulthood. When I completed my work in graduate school, my life was suddenly filled to the brim with exciting activities. I was only thirty years old and opportunities began coming at me faster than I could deal with them. They included a prestigious university position, network television appearances, best-selling books, and national speaking opportunities. I also consulted for five years with President Ronald Reagan about strengthening the institution of the family. After Reagan's second term ended, I consulted occasionally with George H. W. Bush, then George W. Bush.

Those were exciting days. In the early 1980s, I was invited to come to Washington, D.C., to meet with the president of the Mutual Broadcasting System, Marty Rubenstein. He was responsible for the network programming that produced the early *Larry King Show* syndicated on hundreds of radio stations. I was Larry's guest for two hours the following evening, after which Mr. Rubenstein asked me to host my own show as a trial. That occurred on March 25, 1983, when I aired a two-hour talk show heard on six hundred of the larger secular stations. It was sponsored by Purex. Afterward, Mr. Rubenstein offered me a regular "gig" like Larry's program. He looked me in the eye sternly and said, "If you will accept this proposal, I will make you a very wealthy man."

Thank God, I had the sense not to accept the offer. Having a regular radio program fifty-two weeks of the year would have taken me (and my family) over the edge. But the temptation was very strong. My life was at a turning point, and I wavered there for a few days before I realized what was at stake.

All of this high-octane fuel had a downside for my family and me. Early success can be a heady experience for any young man, and I was no exception. I was running at warp speed trying to keep up with all that was happening. I never neglected Shirley or my little girl, Danae, but I did have a tendency to get distracted and overworked. When Ryan came along, I was even more harried. I am embarrassed to say that I once went seventeen nights without being at home with my little family.

My dad observed that I was increasingly absorbed with the trappings of success, and it worried him. He and my mother were on a flight to Hawaii during that time and he had several hours to sit and think. Somewhere over the blue Pacific, he took out a pen and began to write me a letter that was to shape my life. Here is a portion of that letter, written forty-five years ago:

Dear Jimbo

It's been some time since I wrote you a fatherly letter, or a letter of any kind. It is worthy of note, I think, that of all the scores of communications that have made up our total correspondence, including those of your high school and college days, I can recall no letter that had to be written in anger or even in a mild reprimand. They have all had a nostalgic aura of pleasantness. In a word, today I feel more like saying that it has been great to be your father. I am proud to be a member of the team. I am very happy about your success, which is now coming in like showers. It is important for men in all vocations to experience the realizations of their dreams. As this point, you have had a very high ratio of positive returns on your endeavors—almost unbelievable, in fact.

I don't need to remind you that it won't always be so. Life will test you deeply, if only in the ultimate when we have to lay down everything. Until now you have been largely untested, but trials and challenges are inevitable. You should try to prepare for them emotionally because frustration and heartbreak will come your way. I know this is not easy to do in a day of sunshine and roses, but you must try to brace yourself for disappointment.

Then my father came to the gist of his letter. He continued,

We must all pray definitely, pointedly and continuously for your precious daughter. [Ryan had not yet been born.] Danae is growing up in the wickedest section of a world much farther gone into moral decline than the world into which you were born. I have observed that one of the greatest delusions is to suppose that children will be devout Christians simply because

their parents have been. They are also unlikely to be deeply com-
mitted to their faith if their moms and dads have been luke-
warm about spiritual matters. You and Shirley should devote
yourselves wholeheartedly to a deep travail of prayer on behalf
of the children God gives to you. Failure to win them to Christ
would make mere success in your profession a very pale and
washed-out affair, indeed. But this prayer demands time—
time that cannot be given if it is all signed and conscripted and
laid on the altar of career ambition.

In my case, there was a happy coincidence of my career as a
minister with the care of your soul. The modest appointments
that were mine during your childhood provided the time to pray
for you. But in regard to your family, it will have to be done by
design—jealously and fervently guarded. I urge you not to fail
at this point. The tragedy of a child who makes shipwreck of his
or her faith can mar the old age of anyone, Christian or other-
wise. We must all work together to achieve for you the serenity,
which is mine in this respect, as I enter the youth of my old age.
That is only one more reason why we should all drink to the full
the cup that is still in our hands.

Thanks for letting me share my thoughts. Let's talk more when
your mom and I get home.

Your dad

This letter hit me hard because I understood exactly what he
was saying. I have thought about it ever since, and still have the
original copy in my files. In fact, I have memorized portions of
it and still ponder Dad's words. It is apparent now that I almost
made the greatest mistake of my life as a young father. I could

have lost my kids spiritually, as my dad warned. I am thankful that he helped pull me back from the edge.

After reading my father's message and later talking to him about it, Shirley and I began praying earnestly for our daughter, and later for our son. We learned to "fast," which is a biblical concept whereby the pleasure of eating is given up for a time. In our case, that was done one day each week. Even though fasting became difficult for me physically five years later, Shirley continued that practice for more than twenty years. We prayed the same prayer together again and again. It went something like this:

"Heavenly Father, here we are once more with the cry of our hearts. We've come to tell you what you already know, that we care more about the spiritual welfare of our children than any other aspect of our lives. It is more important to us than our health, our work, our reputations, or our possessions. We know there will come a time when our children will be beyond our influence. They will be challenged by the temptations of life. We ask that at that junction between righteousness and unrighteousness, that You place a godly man and woman at that point. Help those influencers to direct them toward the path they should take. Most of all, may the circle be unbroken on the other side of this life, and grant each of us eternal life, which we will celebrate in Your presence forever."

That prayer has been answered wonderfully. Two dedicated mentors came into Danae's and Ryan's lives when they were in college and soon thereafter. Our children have grown up to follow in the footsteps of their forebears, and we enjoy close and fulfilling relationships with them today. Danae has published twenty-four Christian books, most of them for children (including the popular *Woof* series[1]) and Ryan has written five, the latest being *Wanting to Believe*,[2] about his spiritual journey.

I wish I could tell you that I never had another problem with overcommitment, but that would be untrue. It is never easy to change lifelong patterns that are deeply ingrained and established. Men with type A personalities like mine will understand this struggle. My pattern became a roller coaster ride. I would get my workload under control for a time, and then I would gradually begin accepting more and more responsibility. Why? Because, frankly, I'm made to work. The "train" on which I was riding continued to rumble down the track, although at a slower pace than before.

Finally, however, I came to terms with this destructive lifestyle. After praying again one night about numerous invitations and obligations before me, I settled down to read a book called *In-Laws Outlaws*, by counselor Norm Wright.[3] It had nothing to do with my prayer, but there in the second chapter was a Scripture that jumped out at me. It was as though the Lord placed that page in my hands.

The key verses were found in Exodus, Chapter 18, which describes Moses' exhaustion as the leader of Israel. Then his father-in-law, Jethro, came to visit him, much like my father had done for me. Jethro warned Moses that he was working too hard. Here are verses that were relevant to me:

> Now Jethro, the priest of Midian and father-in-law of Moses, heard of everything God had done for Moses and

for his people Israel, and how the LORD had brought Israel out of Egypt.

So Moses went out to meet his father-in-law and bowed down and kissed him. They greeted each other and then went into the tent.

Jethro was delighted to hear about all the good things the Lord had done for Israel in rescuing them from the hand of the Egyptians. He said, "Praise be to the Lord, who rescued you from the hand of the Egyptians and of Pharaoh, and who rescued the people from the hand of the Egyptians."

The next day Moses took his seat to serve as judge for the people, and they stood around him from morning till evening. When his father-in-law saw all that Moses was doing for the people, he said, "What is this you are doing for the people? Why do you alone sit as judge, while all these people stand around you from morning till evening?"

Moses answered him, "Because the people come to me to seek God's will. Whenever they have a dispute, it is brought to me, and I decide between the parties and inform them of God's decrees and laws."

Moses' father-in-law replied, "What you are doing is not good. You and these people who come to you will only wear yourselves out. The work is too heavy for you; you cannot handle it alone. Listen now to me and I will give you some advice, and may God be with you.

"But select capable men from all the people—men who fear God, trustworthy men who hate dishonest gain—and appoint them as officials over thousands, hundreds, fifties and tens. Have them serve as judges for the people at all times, but have them bring every difficult case to you; the simple cases they can decide themselves. That will make your load lighter, because they will share it with you. If you do this and God so commands, you will be able to stand the strain, and all these people will go home satisfied."

Moses listened to his father-in-law and did everything he said.

Then Moses sent his father-in-law on his way, and Jethro returned to his own country. (Exod. 18:1, 7, 9–10, 13–19, 21–24, 27)

Isn't it interesting that the Book of Exodus, which was written nearly 3,600 years ago, is still relevant to our lives today? It is because the biblical text was "God-breathed." It was written by forty authors over a course of 1,500 years, on three continents and in three languages. There has never been another book like the Bible, yet it has been banned in public schools, in most universities, and in the public square.[4] That's where I found the answer to the question I had asked the Lord about an hour earlier.

Let me repeat the verse from Chapter 18 of Exodus that jumped out at me. It reads, "If you follow this advice, and if God commands you to do so, then you will be able to endure the pressures, and all these people will go home in peace" (Exod. 18:23).

I got the message. The next morning, I met with my agent and told him to clear my slate of speaking engagements, except for two events that couldn't be canceled. I accepted the possibility that I would never speak again publicly. However, when executives of Word Publishing heard that I had canceled the citywide seminars, they asked if they could videotape the weekend event that remained. After arguing with them, I agreed to allow cameras to be present.

On September 15–16 of 1977, I spoke to three thousand people in San Antonio, Texas.[5] The video recordings made by Word that weekend became the *Focus on the Family* film series, which was seen by 100 million people in the next ten years.[6] Meanwhile, I stayed at home with my family. Is there any wonder why I believe in the power of prayer?

Later, I resigned from USC and Children's Hospital and opened a humble little two-room office. That was unsettling, but I've never looked back. I started a radio ministry a mile from my home and soon was reaching more people every day than I would have spoken to personally in a lifetime. It was one of those turning points on which the rest of my life would depend.

I wonder if my tendency to run myself ragged when I was younger has also been a problem in your family. I am referring to chronic overcommitment, fatigue, and time pressure. I believe most men have dealt with those circumstances in one way or another. It is an American way of life. Run run run! Puff puff puff! Go go go! Unfortunately, children are the ones who suffer most from a breathless lifestyle. The only way to get off the "crazy train" is to make the tough decisions to slow it down. I know that is easier said than done, but it is worth making the sacrifices necessary to achieve a reasonable pace of living.

Speaking of children, it is now time for us to talk specifically about their spiritual welfare. That's where we're headed.

CHAPTER SEVEN

Apologetics for Kids

"Christian apologetics" refers to the effort to introduce our fellow travelers to the truth of the Scriptures and to the teachings of Jesus Christ. It usually involves evangelism for adults, as taught in Bible study classes and "witnessing" one-on-one. This chapter, however, will address the subject of apologetics for children, primarily as presented by their parents, but also in church school programs and other forms of religious education. It is also called the "spiritual training of children."

As I wrote in the previous chapter, I consider this teaching responsibility to be the highest priority in living for parents and grandparents who are committed Christians. This explains why I have discussed the matter briefly in many of my parenting books. *Your Legacy* is the centerpiece toward which I have been driving. I know there is redundancy in those earlier books, but why wouldn't I address *the* topic again and again if I really believe my own rhetoric? Charles Dickens wrote repeat-edly about social injustice in his books; William Shakespeare focused often on the history of the British monarchy; Stephen Ambrose focused on war and other aspects of American his-tory; and Jane Austen wrote about romantic love. Every writer has his or her central theme. Mine is child development, mar-riage, family, the quest for righteousness, and the salvation of children. Thus, I will articulate my primary message once more for readers who may have missed it.

To understand apologetics, we have to start with the basics. As we know, every good football coach begins his practice ses-sions in August with blocking and tackling, running and kick-ing. These are called "the fundamentals," and they are drilled into players endlessly. Basketball coaches also begin the first day on the court with dribbling, passing, shooting, and defend-ing. This is true for high school freshmen as well as the most seasoned professionals. By the time the first game rolls around, the moves and strategy have become second nature for those who "get it." Those who don't connect continue to ride the bench or they are "cut" from the team.

Learning the fundamentals was similar to what I went through in Army Basic Training. It was nine weeks of trauma, but very effective. Early in the ordeal, a craggy-looking ser-geant with a booming voice held up a rifle and yelled this at us raw recruits:

"This is your friend. If you take care of it, it will take care of you. And don't you ever, ever call it a gun. It is a rifle."

He said it like he meant it. Privates who weren't paying attention were screamed at and sent to KP, which consisted of sixteen miserable hours of kitchen duty. Only the most obtuse recruits referred to a rifle again as a gun.

We spent four hours a day for two weeks learning how take a rifle apart, how to clean it, how to repair it, how to sleep with it, and other stuff that bored me to tears. Most of us lost a nail before learning not to poke our thumbs into a jammed mechanism. I was trying to fix my rifle one day when the bolt slammed into my index finger. Boy! Did that hurt! Everyone else had an "M1 Thumb" for the rest of Basic Training. I was the only one with a black "M1 finger," which was embarrassing to explain. The beat of my heart pounded in that digit for weeks. I still have a groove down the side of my index finger. You can be sure I only made that mistake once.

After all the classroom work, the sergeants marched us to the shooting range and things started to get interesting. I had learned the fundamentals and went on to earn an "expert marksman" rating.

Apologetics is like that. We should start teaching the fundamentals of the faith to children as soon as they can talk. My parents followed that plan. The first word I learned to spell was J-E-S-U-S. When I forgot it, my mother patiently taught it to me again. She told me He was my friend, and that He loved me.

The basics go from there to an understanding of who God is, what He accomplished in Christ, and what He expects us to do. This teaching must begin very early in childhood and continue as the years roll by. Even preschoolers are capable of learning that the flowers, the sky, the birds, and even the rainbows are gifts from God's hand. He made these wonderful things, just as He created each one of us. This is one of the initial lessons in child rearing.

The first Scripture our children should learn is, "God is love" (1 John 4:8). They should be taught to thank Him before eating their food and to ask for His help when they are hurt or scared. Teach them to say elementary prayers, focusing on family members and those who are sick. Read to your children as they grow in maturity from *The Children's Bible* or another simple version. Elaborate on the stories it tells because kids love to hear over and over about biblical characters.

The most effective teaching tool is the modeling provided by parents at home. Children are amazingly perceptive of the things they observe in their parents' unguarded moments. This was illustrated for Shirley and me when our son and daughter were eleven and fifteen. We had gone together to Mammoth Mountain, California, for a ski retreat with another family. Unfortunately, our arrival coincided with a huge blizzard on that Thursday, confining us to the lodge and frustrating the parents and kids alike. Each of us would take turns walking to the window every few minutes in hopes of seeing sunshine that would set us free. It never showed up.

We were also "socked in" on Friday and Saturday, as the storm buried our cars in snow. By that time, the two families were bleary-eyed with cabin fever. Even our dog was getting antsy. However, with the dawn on Sunday morning, wouldn't you know, the sun came streaming into our condo and the sky was a brilliant blue. The snow on the trees was gorgeous and all the ski lifts were up and running. But what were we to do? We had made it a lifelong policy to go to church on Sunday and had chosen not to ski or attend professional athletic events on what we called "the Lord's Day."

One of the Ten Commandments says, "Remember the Sabbath day by keeping it holy. Six days you shall labor and do all your work, but the seventh day is a Sabbath to the Lord your God. On it you shall not do any work, neither you, nor your son or daughter, nor your manservant or maidservant, nor your animals, nor the alien within. For in six days the Lord made the heavens and the earth, the sea, and all that is in them, but he rested on the seventh day. Therefore the Lord blessed the Sabbath day and made it holy" (Exod. 20:8–11).

I learned that lesson as a child and never forgot it. Admittedly, whether to ski or not on Sunday is an individual matter and I'll leave that to my readers to decide. For us, however, the Sabbath is set aside for another purpose. Furthermore, if we skied that morning, we would be causing employees of the ski company to be on the job. Right or wrong, this is what we believe. But that principle came under scrutiny after three days indoors. Everyone wanted to hit the slopes, and to be honest, so did I.

Shirley and I were going bonkers cooped up with all those bored kids. Therefore, I said to my family and friends, "You know, we don't want to be legalistic about this thing [smile]. I think the Lord would grant us an exception in this case. It's such a beautiful day outside. We can have our devotions tonight when we get home from skiing, and I think it would be okay to go."

Everyone was jubilant, or so I thought, and we proceeded to dress for the outing. I finished first and was upstairs to prepare a do-it-yourself breakfast when Shirley came and whispered to me, "You had better go talk to your son." He was always *my* son when there was a problem. I went to Ryan's bedroom and found him crying.

"Goodness, Ryan, what's wrong?" I asked. I will never forget his answer.

"Dad," he said, "I have never seen you compromise before. You have told us it is not right to ski and do things like that on Sunday, but now you're saying it's okay." Tears were still streaming down his cheeks as he talked. "If this was wrong in the past, then it is still wrong today."

Ryan's words hit me like a blow from a hammer. I had disappointed this kid who looked to me for moral guidance. I had violated my own standard of behavior, and Ryan knew it. I felt like the world's biggest hypocrite. After I had regained my composure, I said, "You're right, Ryan. There's no way I can justify the decision I made."

At my request, the two families gathered in the living room again and I related what had happened. Then I said, "I want you all [our guests] to go ahead and ski today. We certainly understand. But our family is going to attend a little church in the village this morning. This is how we spend our Sundays, and today should not be an exception for us."

Members of the other family, both children and adults, said almost in unison, "We don't want to ski today, either. We will go to church with you." And so they did. That afternoon, I got to thinking about what had happened. The next morning, I called my office to say that we would not be returning until Tuesday. Our friends were able to change their schedule, too. So we all went skiing on Monday and had one of the finest days together we have ever had. And my conscience was quiet at last.

This is the point: I had no idea that Ryan had been watching me on that Sunday morning, but I should have anticipated it. Children get their values and beliefs from what they see modeled at home. It is one reason why moms and dads must live a morally consistent life in front of their kids. If they hope to win them for Christ, they can't afford to be casual or whimsical about the things they believe. If you as a parent act as though there is no absolute truth, and if you are too busy to pray and attend church services together, and if your kids are allowed to play soccer or Little League during Sunday School, and if you cheat on your income tax or lie to the bill collector, or fight endlessly with your neighbors, your children will get the message. "Mom and Dad talk a good game, but they don't practice what they preach."

If you serve them such weak soup throughout childhood, they will spew it out when given the opportunity to make their own choices. Any ethical weak spot of this nature—any lack of clarity on matters of right and wrong—will be noted and magnified by the next generation. If you expect your moral and spiritual beliefs to be inherited automatically by your children without intentional training and modeling, just consider the sons of the great patriarchs of the Bible. I'm speaking of Isaac, Samuel, Hezekiah, David, and others. The great priest Eli, who raised Samuel in the synagogue, had two sons named Hophni and Phinehas. Eli was a good man but a passive dad, who didn't take the time to discipline or train his children properly. They grew up to be wicked and rebellious. They consorted with prostitutes in the tabernacle and stole and ate the meat intended for sacrifices.

God pronounced judgment on these two men, and they died on the same day. Their father was so shocked when he heard the news that he fell backward, hit his head on the ground, and died.[1] Most of the patriarchs saw some of their offspring reject God and die outside the faith. That is deeply unsettling to me.

Ministers sometimes fall into the same trap. In the past, it was common for them to believe that if they took care of their churches and fed their flocks, God was obligated to assure the spiritual development of their children. I wish that were true, but it often isn't. The pastor's family is his first mission field, and his evangelism must begin there. It is always tragic when a pastor who loves God and gives his life to the church then fails to bring his own children to a personal relationship with Jesus Christ.

This is what my dad was saying to me when he wrote, "[Your daughter] is growing up in a world much farther gone into moral decline than the world into which you were born." He was helping me realize that my first responsibility was at home, and if I failed there, no other accomplishment would satisfy. It is true for today's parents and grandparents as well. The culture is at war with us for the hearts and minds of our children. Both boys and girls are at maximal risk in a society that encourages teens to engage in the sexual idiocy of the twenty-first century, from binge drinking, to taking illegal drugs, to using pornography, to sex texting, to a host of other sinful behavior.

Though the danger is equally applicable to males and females, this is what I wrote in my book *Bringing Up Girls*:

Let me ask some rhetorical questions to those of you who are raising girls. Do you hope your daughters will be sexually promiscuous even from their early teen years? "Certainly not!" I can almost hear most of you saying. But indulge me for the purposes of illustration. Do you prefer that your girls be brash, loud, and aggressive in their relationships with males?

Do you hope they will be easy marks for boys seeking sexual conquest? Is it your desire that they imitate rogue masculine behavior, such as being quick-tempered, immodest, insensitive, and disrespectful of others? Do you want them to be foulmouthed, crude, rude, profane, and discourteous?

Is it your desire that they dress provocatively in order to attract the attention of guys, revealing more than they conceal? When they become teenagers, do you want them to look like prostitutes, pumping up their lips with collagen and their breasts with silicone? Would you like them to dangle rings from their body parts and dye their hair green, orange, purple, and pink? Do you want them to be so ashamed of their bodies that they feel compelled to diet at nine years of age and are afraid to eat by thirteen? Are you comfortable with professors who will encourage your nearly grown daughters to experiment with lesbian relationships and tell them that bisexuality is an even greater trip? Do you hope that your girls will learn that marriage is an outdated institution that should be redefined or discarded? Do you want them to disdain the cherished spiritual beliefs you have been teaching them since they were babies? If these are your aspirations for your vulnerable little girls, and I'm sure they are not, then you need do nothing to achieve them. The popular culture will do the job for you. It is designed to turn this generation of kids into politically correct little MTV clones.

The influence of the entertainment industry, Madison Avenue, the Internet, hip-hop musicians, some public schools, liberal universities, and other institutions is shaping and warping youngsters and infusing them with harmful ideas that will rob them of the innocence of childhood. As a result, some of our girls will lose their prospects of having a productive and happy marriage. The stability of their future families is hanging in the balance. This is what lies in the paths of children whose parents are overworked, distracted, exhausted, and uninvolved. Without their care and concern, the culture will take them to hell. I have witnessed it a thousand times. Even with proper parental supervision, many of our kids are on the bubble.

I am most concerned about the children among us who are chronically lonely. Their parents are gone much of the time, leaving them to fend for themselves. Human beings desperately need each other, and those who are isolated do not thrive. Not only do lonely children tend to get into trouble, they also become sitting ducks for abusers who understand the emptiness of their souls and use it for their own purposes.[2]

Again, what you teach your kids in the early years is critical. Researcher George Barna confirmed what we have known—that it becomes progressively more difficult to influence children spiritually as they grow older. The data shows that if a person does not accept Jesus Christ as Savior before the age of fourteen, the likelihood of ever doing so is slim. Here are his disturbing findings:

A series of studies we conducted regarding the age at which people accept Christ as their Savior highlights the importance of having people invite Jesus into their hearts as their Savior when they are young. We discovered that the probability of someone embracing Jesus as his or her Savior was 32 percent for those between the ages of 5 and 12; 4 percent for those in the 13–18 age range; and 6 percent for people 19 and older. In other words, if people do not embrace Jesus Christ as their Savior before they reach their teenage years, the chance of their doing so at all is slim.[3]

Specifically, we must do what we can to assure that our boys and girls are established in their faith and have a clear understanding of right and wrong. That is not a generally accepted responsibility. The politically correct ideology contends that all behavior and beliefs are considered equally valid. Nothing is morally wrong and absolute truth doesn't exist. This is called moral relativism and it is the prevailing philosophy in the academic community and in the culture at large. This view holds that children are born good and become corrupt only when they interact with an imperfect society.

Sadly, the concept of sin has no validity for many people because it implies the existence of an eternal Father who judges the affairs of humankind. That makes no sense to unbelievers. We, of course, know and revere Him as the God of Abraham, Isaac, and Jacob. Others are utterly oblivious to Him.

Many churches no longer discuss the concept of sin, choosing instead to focus on positive thinking and that which is "uplifting." Certainly, encouraging words have their place in Christian teaching, but Scripture is explicit on the nature of evil. The Apostle Paul said, "The wages of sin is death" (Rom. 6:23). King David wrote, "Surely I was sinful at birth, sinful from the time my mother conceived me" (Ps. 51:5). Jesus' disciple, John, wrote, "If we claim to be without sin, we deceive ourselves, and the truth is not in us" (1 John 1:8). How can representatives of Christ justify "hopscotching" over basic scriptural principles in this manner?

Here's another question: If nothing is offensive to God, why did Jesus come to this earth? Why did He have to die an agonizing death on the cross? Wasn't it to provide a remedy for sin and depravity? If good and evil don't exist, what exactly *was* the mission of the Messiah? Its meaning is rooted in righteousness, as defined by the eternal God. He holds each of us accountable for it. Someday, "every knee shall bow to me; every tongue confess to God" (Rom. 14:11b). That is what I believe with all my heart, and if you agree, then you should be teaching it to your children.

Let's consider the Scriptures that speak to the issue of spiritual training of children. The first and most explicit instruction is addressed to parents and is found in the book of Deuteronomy. It leaves no wiggle room. This passage is a transcript of the final speech given by Moses to the children of Israel, after he had led them out of Egypt and through forty years of wandering in the wilderness. Only two men who began that journey would live to enter the Promised Land. They were named Joshua and Caleb. The rest would soon die because of their rebellion against Moses and Jehovah.

There were millions of Israelites by that time, and their descendants would soon cross the Jordan River and take possession of the Promised Land. Thus, what we read in the first few chapters of Deuteronomy are the final directions given to those who would fight for and inherit the Land promised to Abraham. It was a historic moment, and every word was given by inspiration to Moses.

It is significant that the first chapter of that speech, quoted in verse 39, was addressed to parents about their children. Moses said, "[They] do not yet know good from bad." That makes my case, doesn't it? Then Moses spoke to the people. Here is his unmistakable message, which echoes down through the ages:

Hear, O Israel: The Lord our God, the Lord is one. Love the Lord your God with all your heart and with all your soul and with all your strength. These commandments that I give you today are to be upon your hearts. Impress them on your children. Talk about them when you sit at home and when you walk along the road, when you lie down and when you get up. Tie them as symbols on your hands and bind them on your foreheads. Write them on the door-frames of your houses and on your gates. (Deut. 6:4–9)

Notice that Moses wasn't simply offering a "suggestion" to parents about the spiritual training of their children. He called that assignment a commandment, and there was urgency in his words. It is not enough to mutter "Now I lay me down to sleep" with your exhausted child at the end of the day. Spiritual teachings are to be on our minds and in our conversation throughout every waking moment. We should look often for opportunities to talk about Jesus and His tender mercies. By the time your sons and daughters are grown, they should have no doubt about the fundamentals of the Christian faith.

There is another rarely quoted Scripture that tells us how God feels about the family. It is written in Malachi 2:15, and states emphatically why the institution of marriage came into existence in the first place.

Has not the Lord made (men and women) one? In flesh and spirit they are his. And why one? Because he was seeking godly offspring. So guard yourself in your spirit, and do not break faith with the wife of your youth.

The institution of marriage was created not for our purposes, but for the Lord's. And why? Because He wanted us to raise our children to be brought up to serve Him. How can we ignore this divine plan?

There are many other Scriptures that emphasize the same instruction. Perhaps the most important is from Psalm 78, which states precisely what God wants parents to do regarding the training of their children. These verses were intended not only for the Children of Israel, but for you and me. This is our assignment. Read these verses very carefully:

O my people, hear my teaching; listen to the words of my mouth. I will open my mouth in parables, I will utter hidden things, things from old—what we have heard and known, what our fathers have told us. We will not hide them from their children; we will tell the next generation the praiseworthy deeds of the Lord, his power, and the wonders he has done. He decreed statutes for Jacob and established the law in Israel, which he commanded our forefathers to teach their children, so the next generation would know them, even the children yet to be born, and they in turn would tell their children. They would put their trust in God and not forget his deeds but would keep his commands. (Ps. 78:1–7)

One generation commends your works to another; they tell of your mighty acts. (Ps. 145:4)

Come, my children, listen to me; I will teach you the fear of the Lord. (Ps. 34:11)

The living, the living—they praise you, as I am doing today; fathers tell their children about your faithfulness. (Isa. 38:19)

Tell it to your children, and let your children tell it to
their children, and their children to the next generation.
(Joel 1:3)

God also said to Moses, "Say to the Israelites, 'The Lord,
the God of your fathers—the God of Abraham, the God of
Isaac and the God of Jacob—has sent me to you.' This is
my name forever, the name by which I am to be remembered from generation to generation." (Exod. 3:15)

These Scriptures are "marching orders" for people of faith.
Again, they are addressed specifically to parents, and all of us
can understand them. No other commandments in the entire
scope of Scripture speak so emphatically to the responsibility
of raising children. That assignment can be summarized by one
verse written by the Apostle Paul in the book of Ephesians. It
says simply, "Bring them up in the nurture and admonition of
the Lord" (Eph. 6:4 KJV).

Now I will share something with you that will explain my
passion for the issue we have been discussing. It espouses a
theological perspective that some of you might not accept. It
has been my lifelong conviction that if a Scripture addresses a
specific issue in straightforward language, it should be accepted
as written. We need look for no other interpretation. The biblical writers said what they meant and meant what they said. So
it is with regard to the certainty of life after death.

When the Creator blew the breath of life into Adam and Eve
in the Garden of Eden, He made them in the image of God.
Respected commentaries interpret that to mean all human
beings were given eternal souls and they will live somewhere
forever. Those who have been "washed" in the blood of Christ

and whose names are written in the Lamb's Book of Life will be in Paradise eternally. Those who reject the gift of forgiveness and salvation will be lost forever, separated from God and His saints. The word "hell" is one of the most frightening and disturbing words appearing in Scripture, but Jesus Himself spoke of it as a literal place. We can't ignore those emphatic words, because they bear the authority of Christ.

This is what is at stake as we set out to introduce our children to the Savior. We can't make their decisions for them, but through prayer and careful guidance, we can influence their choices. The way we handle that responsibility has awesome implications for the future. If our children reach maturity and die without accepting the good news of the gospel, their parents will never see them again in the life to come. That understanding didn't come from me. It is straight from the Word of God. This is the source of the urgency of which I have written.

Now is the time to introduce your children to Jesus Christ. That training should begin early and continue for as long as you have moral authority over them. May the Lord bless you as you fulfill this divine responsibility.

CHAPTER EIGHT

Reaching Our Prodigals

In a conversation with a native of northern Canada some years ago, he described for me the unusual behavior of a bull moose. He said the 1,800-pound animals are made crazy by testosterone and are enraged by anything that enters their territory. When passions are at their peak, and receptive cows are in the neighborhood, it is not uncommon for the beasts to charge anything that moves, even the engines of freight trains as they rumble down the track. Antlers, flesh, hooves, and steel meet head-on in violent collisions. The moose usually lose those encounters, but they don't live long enough to learn anything from the experience.

By a stretch of my fertile imagination, even with tongue in cheek, I see a linkage between the behavior of hotheaded moose and some kids I've known. I've called them "strong-willed children," and they can be tough as nails. From birth or shortly thereafter, they seem to relish conflict with their parents. There's something about being able to irritate and defy powerful adults that whets their appetite for excitement.

In keeping with our theme, we're going to talk in this chapter about the adolescent experience, and especially sons or daughters who are rebellious during that time. They often reject everything their parents have taught and stood for, which has profound spiritual implications for the young person. Clearly, those who are old enough to "sew wild oats" are at particular risk. The way parents react during these times of confrontation can either pull back the prodigal, or drive them farther away. This chapter will address some of those perils and opportunities.

First, I would like for you to read a real-life story about a prodigal son whose mother and father shared it on our *Family Talk* radio and Internet programs. There was a greater response from our listeners to these broadcasts than any in the history of the ministry. Obviously, many parents have dealt with kids who have been extremely difficult to raise. If you are one of those harassed parents or grandparents, pay attention, because this is for you.

With us were Mitch and Windsor Yellen. Their middle child, Zach, who was in Spain during these recordings, granted permission for his parents to discuss his experience. Also with us for the interview was our physician-in-residence and co-host of our broadcast, Dr. Meg Meeker. Ryan Dobson, my son and also a co-host of *Family Talk*, was with us, too. I think you will find this interchange inspirational and informative.

What you are about to read is true. The text has been edited somewhat to change it from the spoken to the written language.

—∾—

JCD: We have some new friends here today that I want to intro-
duce to our listening audience. They are Mitch and Windsor
Yellen, and they own what looks like a castle here in Colorado
Springs. It is called the Pinery. Describe it for us, Mitch.

Mitch: Well, The Pinery is an all-inclusive wedding and event center that provides banquets for our patrons. It includes a Five Dia-
mond restaurant and a private club that overlooks the city. It's
rather like what Ronald Reagan said about America. He called it
"a shining city on a hill." That, we might say, is The Pinery.

JCD: That's a good description. Windsor, I'm going to ask you
to take the lead in telling your family story. Tell us first about
your children.

Windsor: We have a daughter and four sons, and we've been
married for twenty-nine years. Zachariah is the middle child.
He graduated from high school in 2010 and went to Colorado State University that September as a freshman. He came
home for Thanksgiving and asked Mitch and me to sit and talk
with him about something serious. Then he said he was failing all of his classes. To say that we were disappointed would
be an understatement.

JCD: You were paying all of his school bills...

Windsor: Yes, we were. I asked Zach if it was too late to withdraw so that his bad grades wouldn't go on his permanent
transcript. He didn't know the answer, but said that he would
ask the next day. So I said, "Zachariah, I also want you to go to
the registrar's office and withdraw from school and then take
all of the things out of your dorm. Turn in your keys and come
back home to Colorado Springs."

Zach did that. This was the day before Thanksgiving.

JCD: Had he been a rebellious kid?

Windsor: No, he'd been pretty easy. He had lettered in two varsity sports. He was the kicker for the football team and the goalie for the soccer team. He had decent grades at a tough high school. Actually, he was always a sweet-natured child. He was helpful. His middle name is Benjamin, and in Hebrew that means, "right-hand man." That really did describe Zach. If you were having problems with electronic devices, he generally knew how to help. That's why we were surprised when he did poorly in school.

JCD: His personality must have changed radically. Is that right, Mitch?

Mitch: It is. We were not fully aware at the time that he was doing drugs. We just knew that there was a darkness in his spirit. It was like a light being dimmed. I hear that from other parents of kids on drugs. They ask, "Where did my son go?"

JCD: Was he drinking and smoking and running around with the wrong crowd?

Mitch: Yes, and there was nothing we could really do about it.

Windsor: When he came back to Colorado Springs right before Thanksgiving Day, Zach didn't come home that night or return my calls to his cell. He was very rebellious. I was awake through the night praying and asking God for wisdom. I was also crying a lot and saying, "Lord. I'm scared for my son. I don't know what to do. I just need more wisdom than I have."

Mitch and I were getting up every morning and praying together, but I wasn't able to get any restful sleep. So after a couple of nights of not returning my calls, I said, "Zachariah, you cannot live here if you are going to rebel against the rules of our house." I said, "It's one thing to rebel, but when it's right in my face, I would rather pray for you and put you in God's hands." It was terrifying to me.

JCD: I understand Zach had two younger siblings who were watching their brother. You were concerned about them, too.

Windsor: Yes. Abraham and Eli were watching. And it was tough. The next day, he didn't honor his curfew. He showed up the next afternoon when I was in his bedroom. I was furious and troubled at the same time. I wanted to scream at him, but I was able to control my anger and I said, "You have to go."

JCD: And you were very hurt.

Windsor: Yes. Very hurt. I took it personally. But I remember one of the things I learned from you was not to threaten something that I wasn't going to do. I didn't say, "If you do this again I'll kill you," because obviously I wouldn't do that. But I did ask him to leave.

So I was in his bedroom and I started pulling things out of his drawer and setting them on the floor. And I said, "Anything you leave behind I'm going to give away, and I'm going to turn your room into a guest room."

I was that upset. And he said, "You'll never do that." And I said, "Zachariah, you need to go." At one point I looked at Zach and said, "If you're going to ruin your life, I'm not going to watch." I turned off his cell phone and took away the keys to his car. Then I walked him to the front door and shut it behind him. I watched him from the front window. He went to the end of the driveway and then waited. I started crying and praying, and I saw a friend pick him up and they drove away.

JCD: Was that the most difficult moment of your life?

Windsor: It was the second most difficult. The most stressful was on Christmas Day, a month later.

Mitch: We let him come home on Christmas Eve, and we had a wonderful dinner at a good restaurant. We gave him a curfew that night, but he never came home.

Windsor: The next day was Christmas. I was making dinner and I was very sad. It was just a horrible feeling hanging over all of us. The five of us all missed him. We didn't know what was going on because he didn't have his phone. And he didn't have his car.

Then, the doorbell rang. I went to the door and the rest of the family was leaning over my right shoulder. There was Zach. And I said, "Zachariah, are you ready to obey the rules of this house?"

He said, "No. I just came to see what you got me for Christmas." And I said, "Nothing. God bless you." And I shut the door. That was the hardest thing I've ever experienced in my life. I felt like I was going to be sick.

JCD: To send your son away, whom you had brought into the world, and to do it on Christmas Day had to have been heart-wrenching. You had tried to teach him about the Lord and thought he had accepted and understood what that meant. But then Zach showed up at the door just to see what you had bought him. That was disrespectful and cruel. Obviously, Zach was saying that he had no intention of following your leadership, and that he was going to continue using drugs and defying the rules of the house. That must have been devastating to you both.

Windsor: It was that and more. Zach admitted that he was smoking, drinking, and taking pills. I didn't know what else he was doing, but he was just not the same person.

JCD: What happened next?

Windsor: My boys looked at me and said, "You are so mean— it's Christmas Day. You are so mean."

I ran up to my bedroom and went into the closet. I cried like I can't ever remember crying before, and I said, "Lord, I need your help. I just need help." Eventually, I came out and washed my face, and of course, it was swollen and I had red eyes. I came downstairs and it was literally the worst Christmas dinner in the history of the world. I was sniffling and tear-stained. My kids and Mitch were so sad. We were just sitting there, and no one felt like eating. It was just awful.

JCD: Mitch, did you also think at that time that Windsor was the meanest woman in the world?

Mitch: Oh, no! I knew she was right. But I was the parent who didn't have the courage to respond properly. I didn't want to see Zach just walk out the door, so I asked him, "Where can I drop you off?" He wanted me to take him to a neighborhood I didn't recognize. When he got out of the car, I told him I loved him and that I'd be praying for him. I just had to trust God at that point.

JCD: Windsor, you really didn't know if you'd ever see your son again.

Windsor: I didn't, and I knew his behavior was dangerous. When Zach was a little guy and we gave him Superman or Batman jammies, he jumped off the back of the sofa with his arms stretched out. He landed on the hardwood floor and knocked himself out because he thought he could fly. He was a daredevil and he took chances. I knew that he would take risks out there on his own, and that scared me, too.

JCD: Well, continue with the story. What happened next?

Windsor: The following week, Mitch and I kept praying and fasting together and asking God for direction. We believed He had a plan for Zach and that His hand was on him. Our prayer has been that he would come home and apologize and straighten up. But he couldn't continue to drink and do drugs and be rebellious and irresponsible. We decided to make no contact with our son. I even had the locks changed so that Zach couldn't sneak in and help himself to whatever was there. That was a very tough time and I just depended on the Lord to get us through it.

JCD: I admire you, Windsor. You are a very courageous lady. You did the right thing, but I don't know many mothers who could have remained firm at a time like that. It must have torn your heart out.

Windsor: The afternoon of New Year's Day, Zach knocked on the door. He was very somber and he said, "Mom, I will do whatever you ask. May I please come back to the house?" And I said, "Yes. You can come in as long as you obey the rules."

That was in January, and from then until August he worked for The Pinery catering. He drove a van, getting up sometimes at four thirty or five in the morning, putting on a uniform, and delivering food. He sometimes fell asleep sitting straight up on our sofa after coming in at night. He was exhausted. His job required heavy lifting and hard work. Catering is not for the faint of heart. It's precise and there are many people to please.

JCD: Was he playing by the rules at that point?

Windsor: Well, yes, but he kept asking, "What do I have to do to go back to college so that you will pay for it? What do I have to do so you will trust me?"

I wasn't really sure what to tell him. At two a.m. I went to the family room downstairs because I couldn't sleep. I was sitting at our desktop computer and I said, "Lord, could you please send me an e-mail? Could you make it plain? I'm a broken human being, and I want so much to do the right thing. But I don't know what the right thing is. I need help."

I went to the Google search bar, and I typed in something absurd. I think it was "help for rebellious children who won't listen to their parents." Right across the screen came the letters, NOLS, which stood for "National Outdoor Leadership School." They take students to places all over the world, for college credit or not, and the campers were as young as fifteen years old. It's for young people who want to learn about the outdoors. They also take kids who are struggling away from friends who are a bad influence—and put them in the wilderness. One of their programs was in the Rocky Mountains, beginning in Lander, Wyoming. It started in September and offered sixteen units of college credit. They would be gone until the first part of December.

Zach would be in the Rocky Mountains with thirteen of his "closest friends"—meaning people he didn't know—with three leaders. Each participant carried a fifty-five-pound pack, but could take no drugs, no cigarettes, no alcohol, no laptop, and no phone. It was just Zach and the wilderness. So I told him, "If you will complete and finish that wilderness program properly, and you won't drop out, and you do get the credits, Dad and I will trust you with another semester at CSU."

Zach agreed and worked at The Pinery until time to leave. He was supposed to have quit smoking and begin running and lifting weights to get in shape. He needed to buy his boots early and wear them often. Zachariah went to REI one week before he left and bought his boots. He never ran once. He didn't quit smoking until he put the last cigarette out right before he went through the doors to meet his leader. He didn't really prepare himself at all.

Two weeks before he was supposed to leave, he didn't come home one night. He had been doing so well. Mitch and I woke up at six a.m. and began to pray because he wasn't in his bedroom. He had a friend down the road, so we drove to his house. Zach's car was parked in front. We just stretched our hands out toward the house and prayed for him.

Mitch: I got a call from Zach at about three thirty in the afternoon saying, "Dad, I think I need to go to the emergency room." And I said, "What's going on?" He started describing an injury to me. It didn't sound all that bad so I told him, "Well, just go ahead and call your mom, honey. I'm in a meeting." If it was an emergency I told him I would come, so he called his mother.

Windsor: I said, "Zach, do you need stitches?" And he said, "Well I was on my long board last night on Cresta Road, and I was crouching down and I hit a pothole." And he said, "I think I need some stitches in my forearm."

I said, "Okay, honey, well how many stitches?" And he said, "I don't know. I wrapped a T-shirt around my arm and the blood stuck to it. If I pull it off it will really hurt."

I got home and he basically told me what he had been doing. He was on a long board, and he had one leg up and one leg down.

JCD: Ryan, help us understand. Is that a big skateboard?

Ryan: It is.

Mitch: Zach was going about thirty-five miles per hour.

Windsor: The accident happened at two a.m. He was "loaded" and the front right part of the board hit the pothole. He put out his right elbow and it took all of the force of his fall. It was the most horrendous wound. I took his forearm and put it over the sink and soaked it. He was sitting on a stool, and he wouldn't even look at it. He said, "Mom, it's making me sick."

I took a peek and I could see his bone and the tendons, and it was really ugly. And so I told him, "Okay, buddy, we are going to Memorial Hospital." I put him in the car and started praying.

We got to the hospital and we waited a long time in Emergency. Then they took him into one of the triage rooms, and the doc came in and immediately started scrubbing all of the road rash and debris out of the wound.

JCD: Rocks and dirt and…

Windsor: …and tar. It was just hideous. That kind of injury would normally have made me sick, but it didn't because I was focused on Zach. The doctor was making small talk with him and he asked, "What are your plans?"

Zach said, "Well, in two weeks I'm going to the National Outdoor Leadership School in Lander, Wyoming, for three months in the wilderness."

The doctor said flat out, "Oh, no, you're not!" And Zach said, "Oh, yes, I am." And the doctor said, "Do you want to lose your arm? This is a really bad wound. You need to let it heal, and you could lose your entire arm if it gets infected." Then he said, "I need to get some more sutures, I will be back in a minute."

It was just Zachariah and me in the room. He isn't a crybaby—he's a tough guy—but he looked at me. He cursed under his breath and then one huge tear rolled down his cheek.

JCD: Is that the first time you have seen him cry since he grew up?

Windsor: Yes. Zach said, "I can't believe I did this to myself." And I said, "Zachariah, you will go on that trip." And he said, "I don't believe that." I said, "Well, I have enough faith for the two of us."

Two seconds later his dad came through the door and said almost exactly what I had said. He looked right at Zach and said, "You *will* go. God will close that wound, and you *will* go."

Mitchell just prayed "heaven" down, and took his hand and told him how much he loved him. He told Zach that God had a future and a hope for him, and that it was not over.

Zach told us that moment in the hospital was the turning point for him.

JCD: The reason that experience made such an impact on Zach, as I interpret it, is because he saw his mom and dad's compassion. He knew you loved him, even though he didn't deserve it—and even though he had thrown your efforts to help him back in your faces. He had violated everything you had taught him and took drugs that were harming his body. Despite all that, he recognized that his mom and dad were still on his team. That is love.

Windsor: You're right. For two weeks he didn't leave the house. He said he quit taking drugs but couldn't give up cigarettes because he was addicted to them. He said he tried to slow down a little because he knew that soon he wouldn't have cigarettes in the wilderness. A couple weeks later, we piled into the car and headed for Lander, Wyoming, and went to the Noble Hotel, which is the jumping-off place. We had dinner together—Zach was really quiet.

Ryan: How long was his trip going to be again?

Windsor: They started in September and ended in December.

Mitch: It would take ninety-four days and we knew we wouldn't hear from him during that time.

Windsor: With that, Zach packed up and headed into the wilderness.

JCD: I think you told us that he almost gave up and quit.

Windsor: Yes, that almost happened on his second day in the wilderness. He said because he didn't quit smoking and didn't get in shape, he was unprepared for the physical stresses of the trip. He said out of the fourteen students who were hiking, there was only one person behind him. Only pride kept him from letting that lagging hiker get ahead of him on the trail. He just kept thinking in his head, "I cannot be last. I cannot be that guy."

And so his competitive nature kicked in and helped him a bit. The second day it rained like he couldn't believe. As they kept ascending, fog rolled in and his leader lost his bearings. They got up high enough in elevation where the rain turned to snow. Zach had failed to put his things inside a plastic bag in the backpack. So everything was sodden and frozen and soaked and the stuff became heavier the farther they walked. Finally they made camp.

One of the cardinal principles that NOLS lives by is to "leave no trace behind." Since they couldn't find their campsite, there wasn't a suitable place to light a fire. The packers couldn't put a burn scar where there hadn't been one before. So they were freezing.

The guys didn't know how to put up their tent, and their leader wanted to make it a teachable moment so he didn't help them. Zach's memory is of sitting up with his wet tent hitting his cheek, and not getting very much sleep. So the next day he was so frustrated and tired that when they got to the campsite, he ripped his backpack off his back. When he did, the strap caught his arm and opened up the wound.

JCD: And there was no emergency medical help on the mountain.

Windsor: There was no treatment available except scalding hot water. So every day, his leader shot a syringe of scalding water into the wound and re-bandaged it. Zach said it was awful.

Ryan: I think you call that tough love, Dad.

JCD: That's exactly what it was, Ryan. It's like Boot Camp for Marine recruits at Parris Island. They go in as undisciplined, whiny, lost kids, and come out as Marines. It assaults the entire system, but it builds character and strength.

Windsor: So September, October, and November went by, and I'm really missing my son, especially on Thanksgiving—remembering the horrible time we had the year before. I was in the kitchen one night during the first week of December—and my cell phone rang. The caller ID indicated it was Zach, and I was shocked because I knew he was in the wilderness.

I couldn't imagine who had his phone. I said, "Hello," and Zach said, "Hey, Ma!" I was so happy to hear the way he said it, I could tell there was already something different.

I said, "Zach, where are you?" And he said, "Well we're in the red rocks outside of Las Vegas. We can see the lights, and we can get a cell signal." He said, "Mom, I just have a few minutes before we have a team meeting, but I want to ask you a question." I said, "Sure, shoot." He said, "If you were going to read your Bible, where would you start?"

Praise the Lord for my husband who stuck a tiny New Testament in his backpack, unbeknownst to Zach at the time. He must have found it. So I said, "Well if it were me, I would read the Gospel of John." And he said, "Okay, I have to go, but they're going to let me contact you again later tonight and I'll call you."

JCD: Was your heart just thumping?

Windsor: It was pounding! So I called Mitch and we prayed through that afternoon. We waited and prayed and waited and prayed. When the phone rang a few hours later, I said, "Hello? Hello?" And this sweet voice said, "Ma?"

"Yes, Zachariah."

He said, "I need help." I said, "Zach, everybody needs help, honey."

And he said, "Would you pray for me?"

And I said, "Zachariah, do you want me to pray for you, or do you want to ask Jesus into your heart?" And he said, "Yes."

So I led my son in the sinner's prayer, and that was the best day of my life.

JCD: I have a lump in my throat.

Windsor: Zachariah is so different. He has never looked back from that day. He came up the escalator at DIA with this blowing mane of hair and this beautiful smile on his face. Zach has beautiful blue eyes, and they were just shining. And you know it's not as though every struggle ends when you ask Jesus into your heart. It is the "road less traveled," and we do struggle to become more like the Lord. But it's just that God met him in such a sweet way out there. He said that so many times he felt completely alone, and as he turned in his sleeping bag at night—looking up at the stars—he just knew. He said he just couldn't help but know that God was there, and you wouldn't think that he would understand that, but he did.

JCD: And Jesus knew. When you were praying and it seemed as though He wasn't listening, He was close enough to touch. Sometimes all you hear in a crisis is, "Trust me." But the Lord misses nothing. When you were calling out to Him in your fear and agony, He led you to the Internet site, where you learned about the wilderness program. The Holy Spirit was also with Zach when he was lying under the stars and felt the call to surrender his heart. I experienced it, too, at a high school summer camp, and it was a wonderful thing. I asked you, Windsor, if you would tell this story because I wanted our listeners to hear your compassion. Now let's hear it from you, Mitch. What was going on inside you during this ordeal?

Mitch: My heart was breaking during the worst of it. I couldn't sleep at night. I was just tossing and turning the whole time. I prayed for Zach since he was a little boy. I led him through the sinner's prayer when he was six or seven, like many fathers do with their sons. But I had faith, and I believed that God would turn him around and that he would take hold spiritually. I asked that Zach's faith would become new again.

JCD: It's significant that you have five children, but only one became a prodigal. Zach was the child you lay awake at night thinking and praying about. He was your lost sheep. Luke 15 describes a shepherd who had a hundred sheep under his protection, and one of them wandered away. The shepherd left the ninety-nine to search for the one that was lost. In the same way, you were trying to save the boy who was in trouble.

Mitch: That's *exactly* what we were doing. Zach was in trouble. We pray for all our kids, but we were interceding and fasting and petitioning God to turn this middle son around.

JCD: Now there's more to this story, but I want to get Ryan and Doctor Meeker in on the conversation. Ryan, do you see any similarities with your own experience at about the same time of your life?

Ryan: Absolutely. My story parallels Zach's in some ways. I didn't like school and I didn't want to go to college. I had a good job—it paid *cash*. I could see what I had accomplished at the end of the day. But my folks wanted me to get an education, and so I went. I wasn't in rebellion. I was just playing around and making bad grades. My heart wasn't in it.

When Dad saw my grades, he called and said, "You know, Ryan, we can't waste God's money. If you make another D, you call me." We weren't angry at one another. It was just a quiet conversation man-to-man. By this time, I liked being at college but still wasn't doing well there. A few months later, I called my dad to tell him I got another D, and he said, "Well, Ryan, it's over. Drop out of school and figure out what you're going to do with your life. You can't come home because that would be too easy. Find a place to live and get a job. Maybe you can flip hamburgers or find another way to feed yourself."

I've never been so shocked my life. I knew my dad wanted me to get an education, but he cut off the money and pulled me out of school. I hung up the phone and it was like the weight of the world was on me. I was scared and had no plan for what would come next.

I drove back to Colorado Springs, which was the worst place to go because the economy was very depressed at the time. I really didn't know if I could survive. I chose the Springs because I figured, "I had better be near my parents because I don't think they would let me starve or want to see me living in a gutter."

I looked everywhere for a job and finally found work as a bus boy making five dollars an hour. I was lucky to get it. More than three hundred people had applied for that job. Fully-credentialed chefs applied just to get their foot in the door. I rented a one-hundred-year-old cabin for a hundred dollars per month and my Dad paid the first and last month's rent. The cabin was a wreck. It was leaning and a complete mess. It's all I could afford.

Dad, tell everyone what happened next.

JCD: It was a scary time for all of us. Pulling Ryan out of school was the most difficult thing I've ever had to do. It was fraught with danger. I knew he might never get back on course and could have wrecked his life. He might have become a street person or something worse. He was at a crisis point, and we were praying daily for him.

About six months later, Ryan was at our house for dinner and he and I were talking afterward. I'll never forget that moment. He said, "Dad, those people I'm working with are going nowhere. They are absolutely lost."

I said, "I know, Ryan. That's what happens if you don't prepare yourself for a better life."

Then I said, "Would you like one more shot?"

He didn't know what I meant and he said, "One more shot at what?"

I'll say with a smile that Ryan must have thought I was going to shoot him. I said, "Another shot at college. I'm thinking about giving you another chance, but only for one semester. If you apply yourself, I'll approve another term. But if you play around again, you'll be on your own."

Ryan looked at me in disbelief. He couldn't believe what he was hearing. He took the challenge and enrolled at Biola University. He went on to graduate from there and I spoke at his graduation ceremony. Here he is today. He is the author of five books, is a very accomplished speaker and teacher, and has a wonderful little family. I am very proud of him. And now we have the privilege of working together at *Family Talk*. Just like you, Mitch and Windsor, the Lord walked us through our time in the valley and answered our fervent prayers.

Doctor Meeker, what are you thinking?

MM: As I listened to these stories, especially yours, Windsor, I was asking myself, "Could I have done what you did? Would I, as the mother of *my* twenty-one-year-old son, have had the courage to pack his bags and tell him to leave? Would I have ushered him to the front door on Christmas Day and closed it behind him? I don't know if I could have done it, and that is why I admire your strength.

When your kids said to you, "Mom, you're being so mean," I'm sure you felt mean. But look at who Zach called from that mountaintop overlooking the lights of the city. He phoned you, the "mean one," because he trusted you and knew you loved him. What a wonderful lesson for the mothers listening to us. You, Windsor—the one who threw your son out—were the one he reached out to for comfort.

I'm reminded of Proverbs 22:6 that says, "Train up a child in the way he should go, and when he is old he will not depart from it" (NKJV). We as moms don't naturally think of training our children; we tend to think of loving, and nurturing, and being kind, and giving them things, and making life easy for them. But the responsibility of training is gritty. It's hard. It's painful. There is nothing easy about it. But you did it, and I applaud you!

Windsor: I really have to give all the credit to the Lord for whispering to my heart when I really needed to hear from Him. That's what I've learned to do. When I am afraid, I trust in the Lord and He is always there. He loves our kids more than we do. They belong to Him, and He loans them to us for a short season to raise them to the best of our ability.

JCD: All of us are prodigal children when it really comes down to it. We all have disobeyed the Father.

Windsor: Yes. I have made many mistakes. I've spoiled our kids at times, and I've been sharp and angry at other times. I've screamed at them and acted horribly. I have had successes and I've had failures. But, you know, His mercies are new every morning. He's faithful, and if we just confess our faults and ask for His help, He will forgive and heal. If I could encourage our listeners, I'd say don't give up. Continue to pray and fast. It will come around in the end.

Mitch: You know, if I could just share something with fathers. Windsor and I knew we were dealing with spiritual darkness in our home, and so we put on the armor of God every morning before we went into battle. We knew we had to fight for the soul of our son, and that we couldn't prevail against evil in our own strength.

JCD: Mitch, we have complimented Windsor for her courage in this situation, but you deserve our applause, too. You were not the disciplinarian, but you knew your role was to support your wife. You did it well.

Mitch: Frankly, I was scared—scared to send Zach into the world alone, but I knew standing with Windsor was the right thing to do.

Windsor: Mitch did affirm me in my darkest hours. His eyes were filled with tears and he was very sad. But I knew he was standing with me.

JCD: If Mitch hadn't provided that support when your kids were critical of you, Windsor, he would have destroyed your authority and weakened your confidence. Mitch, tell us about your childhood and why it gave you a tender spirit. You were raised in a very permissive home, weren't you?

Mitch: My mother abandoned us when I was eleven and my father was a workaholic. I was on my own from then on.

JCD: So you didn't have a lot of parental love?

Mitch: Not a lot of parental love.

JCD: And that made it difficult for you to confront. Well, in light of that, I think it is commendable how supportive you were of Windsor as she went through her trial by fire.

MM: Windsor, I know there are mothers out there who have pre-adolescent or adolescent sons or daughters. There is a mother listening today who has a fourteen- or fifteen-year-old who is very rebellious and taking drugs or crossing all the boundaries at home and in school. What do you recommend to her? She is afraid to confront her child because she might drive her child away. Will you speak directly to that mom? Because there are so many like her.

Windsor: The first thing I would suggest is to ask God to give her Scriptures that she can pray over her kids. The verse that He gave Mitch and me was Colossians 1:9, which reads:

> For this reason, since the day we heard about you, we have not stopped praying for you. We continually ask God to fill you with the knowledge of his will through all the wisdom and understanding the Spirit gives.

> We prayed that verse every day because we knew we didn't have the wisdom to handle our family situation. Then I asked God to show me the things my kids cared about most that I could use to get them to play by the rules.

> Every son or daughter has something that is valued very highly. For some it's their phones; for others it's video games or a sport they love to play, or friends that they spend time with. It is really important to know what it is that lights your kid's fire and then to be willing to use those privileges as leverage when they are rebelling. You have to have some measure of control. Empty words just don't work because teenagers don't care about that.

> Another suggestion is to pray *with* another person. Jesus said, "If two of you shall agree on earth as touching anything

that they shall ask, it shall be done for them of my Father which is in heaven."[1] That's a promise.

You know there is also power in praising God through difficulty. You have to surrender to Him and say, "Even though we don't understand, we trust You." That pleases the Lord.

Finally, I believe in *fasting* and prayer. Jesus didn't say, "*If* you fast…" He said "*When* you fast." He assumed we would do it.

MM: I would like to ask Mitch a question. To the dad out there whose kids are in serious trouble, what advice can you offer him?

Mitch: Having the kind of background that I've had, there wasn't a strong training ground for me to know what to do. You know when children come along, there is no playbook that spells out what to do. Windsor took the lead initially and I followed her. But what I learned over the years, as I read your books, Doctor Dobson, is that as painful as it is for me to say "No" to my son or daughter, or to set definite curfews for them, I knew you had to do it. Don't bend in that moment of crisis. There are times when you have to be tough. Even if they lash out and say, "I hate you" or "I'm so angry at you," you're the dad and you have to stand firm. Then you keep loving them unconditionally. That is what Windsor and I did, and our son came back when he heard the voice of the Lord.

MM: Yes! If you don't stand firm, you destroy that young man or woman. I have a Facebook page at *Family Talk*, which includes a regular feature called, "Ask Dr. Meg." Parents call me and ask about how to handle children as young as seven, eight, or nine. These little kids are already out of control. They are disrespectful, won't mind, and even swear at their parents. Moms will say to me, "There's not a thing I can do to control them." Of course there is! Parents have the authority to rein in their rebellious kids, but it takes courage to do it. They can't stay alive without us, especially elementary school children. Instead, many parents yield their position of power to their kids and allow them to go wild. They are crippling their children when they do that.

JCD: I agree emphatically, Meg. A question I have been asked often by parents, usually by mothers, is a variation on this theme: "I have a nineteen-year-old son who is sullen and disrespectful to his dad and me. He is running with the wrong crowd, he sleeps until noon, and won't even look for a job. He uses foul language and all he wants to do is watch TV or play video games. He won't even take out the trash or make his bed. He also has pornography in his room. He might even be taking drugs, but I don't know. I haven't asked. We are scared of him and just don't know what to do." The details differ, but this is a typical situation. Then this mom says, "He makes our lives miserable."[2]

I usually say, "I will offer you three words of advice: 'Help him pack.' He wants you to fix his meals, wash his clothes, put up with his snide comments, provide insurance, put a roof over his head, pay for his car, and on it goes. If you support this lazy, disrespectful son or daughter, you have become an enabler for this young man or woman. Because you love him, you are making it possible for your son to waste his life and squander opportunities to get himself together. His rocket is sitting on the launch pad, but it isn't firing. Again, I suggest you put his stuff on the front porch and tell him it's time to get acquainted with the real world."

This is what Windsor did, in essence. She sent Zach packing. It was the best thing she could have done, and he knew it.

MM: We should talk also about the single mother who is trying to deal with a rebellious kid or two or more. I am very concerned about her. She has been at a disadvantage since her children were young. She only sees them half the time, and her husband may be counteracting everything constructive she has tried to do. This mom is afraid to confront her youngster because he or she might choose to live with a permissive father who has no rules. I hear from these mothers often and my heart goes out to them.

JCD: I hear from them, too, Meg. I've said many times that the single mother who is struggling to earn a living and raise healthy kids, too, has the toughest job in the universe. The rest of us should do everything we can to give her a hand. We'll have to talk about that on another program.

Our time is gone for today, but let me say to you, Mitch and Windsor, how much we appreciate you being willing to share your intimate story with our listeners. Please thank Zach, also, for allowing us to discuss his experience. The next time he is home, I would love to get acquainted with him. He is going to land squarely on his feet and I'd like to shake his hand.

Blessings to you all.

Mitch and Windsor: We'll tell Zach, and thanks so much for having us.

Later

This conversation with the Yellen family was very inspirational to me. I hope you enjoyed it, too. Let me offer some observations and conclusions about what we have heard. At first I thought Zach was a classic strong-willed individual, but clearly he was not. As his mother told us, he was a sweet boy until he graduated from high school. He hit the skids afterward because he fell in with the wrong friends and wandered into drugs and alcohol. This combination can totally redirect the values, motivation, and personality of anybody, especially a boy who is under the influence of surging testosterone. I would also guess that something significant happened to Zach when he was at the university. I don't know that story, but something apparently changed his thought process.

You'll remember that Mitch quoted a man who said, "Where did my son go?" Millions of parents have asked the same question. They say, "Overnight, my kid became someone I hardly recognized." Once a teen or young adult begins to party and take mind-altering drugs, strange behavior is the order of the day. It obviously took its toll on Zach. Why would an intelligent guy get on a long board in the middle of the night and burn along at thirty-five miles an hour? The answer is that he was "loaded," as he admitted to his mother. I guess it was inevitable that he would hit *something*. His judgment wasn't firing on all cylinders.

I join Mitch and Windsor in thanking God for Zach's turnaround. What actually accounted for it? The answers to that question may be useful to those of my readers who are still dealing with a wayward son or daughter.

Zach had four assets that worked in his favor. First, he had a strong, caring, intact family. Mitch and Windsor loved all their children, and each of them knew it. These parents served as an anchor when Zach's boat was rocking and reeling.

Second, Mitch and Windsor knew prayer was what they needed most. I believe the Lord honored their fasting and prayers and brought their son "home."

Third, Zach had a spiritual foundation on which his repentance and renewal were eventually based. Mitch had led his son into a relationship with Jesus Christ when he was a very young child. That early teaching became priceless when the crisis occurred.

Finally, Mitch was a very good and loving father, but he may not have fully understood the principles of "love must be tough." There is a time for accountability and strength. That experience required not only loving kindness, but also toughness. They work best when they operate in tandem.

Being tough in the context of love is called for, such as when a husband or wife is having an affair, or is an unrepentant alcoholic, or is bankrupting the family with a gambling addiction, or is deeply involved in pornography. The spouse who is behaving irresponsibly and disrespectfully needs the strength and conviction of the other spouse to help make the difficult choices, even though it is fiercely opposed. Appeasement and weakness DO NOT WORK in human affairs. That is the lesson of history.

Prime Minister Neville Chamberlain flew to Munich in 1938 to meet with the German Chancellor, Adolph Hitler. The brutal dictator wanted to seize Czechoslovakia and enslave its people. He promised no more territorial claims if the British government would not oppose the takeover. Chamberlain agreed and flew back to London. He is still seen on film today waving a paper signed by Hitler, and claiming, "Peace in Our Time."[3] What followed was the brutalization of the Czechoslovakian people and five years of bitter world war during which fifty million people died. Chamberlain set it up by appeasing a mass murderer.

This is also true for teens who regularly come home drunk at three a.m., vomit in the bathroom, and are unable to work the next day. Such a young man or woman is in deep trouble and needs to be confronted by tough parents. To pacify an adolescent who behaves like this and to dole out money to keep the peace is to become an enabler. That will cripple him or her in time.

I don't know if Windsor had read my book *Love Must Be Tough*,[4] but she understood intuitively the principles it espoused. Even though it was terribly distressing to confront her beloved son, she had the courage to say, if I can paraphrase, "I can't stop you from wrecking your life, but I certainly don't have to watch it happen." Then she said unequivocally, "Let's pack."

Let me say it a different way. Tough love is what is needed most when someone you care for deeply, whether it is a spouse or an offspring, is behaving irrationally and foolishly. A parent (Windsor in this case) must react with firmness, courage, conviction, and passion. There can be no indecision in that time of confrontation. That is exactly what Windsor provided. She didn't scream insults or hurl empty threats. Her reaction was a classic case of tough love in action.

As Doctor Meeker said, there are very few moms who could have handled that horrible moment as well. That's why we all commended her for it. The tough love didn't stop there. It continued until Zach realized he had made a mess of his life, and called from the mountain to say, "Would you pray for me?"

Windsor replied, "Zachariah, do you want me to pray for you, or do you want to ask Jesus into your heart?" And he said, "Yes."

That was the loving part of the relationship. Windsor didn't berate her son and tell him how badly he had hurt her and the family. No, she showed compassion and motherly love to her son.

Another component of "love must be tough" is that it is most successful in a crisis. That's when change is most likely to occur. It doesn't happen when two agitated and angry people are engaged in a collision of wills. The "coming together" usually happens later, when conviction and compassion interact. Again, Windsor responded like the Christian mom she is. She asked for guidance from the Holy Spirit and received it.

To illustrate further, let's read the parable of the Prodigal Son, told by Jesus and recorded in Luke 15:11–32. You will see how this story coincides with what we read in the Yellens' experience. Though the Scripture and Jesus' words are not referred to as "tough love," that is exactly what I would call them. You'll see why as we review the story:

A man had two sons. When the younger told his father, "I want my share of your estate now, instead of waiting until you die!" his father agreed to divide his wealth between his sons. A few days later this younger son packed all his belonging and took a trip to a distant land, and there he wasted all his money on parties and prostitutes.

About the time his money was gone a great famine swept over the land, and he began to starve. He persuaded a local farmer to hire him to feed his pigs. The boy became so hungry that even the pods he was feeding the swine looked good to him. And no one gave him anything. When he finally came to his senses, he said to himself, "At home even the hired men have food enough to spare, and here I am dying of hunger! I will go home to my father and say, 'Father, I have sinned against both heaven and you, and am no longer worthy of being called your son. Please take me on as a hired man.'"

So he returned home to his father. And while he was still a long distance away, his father saw him coming, and was filled with loving pity and ran and embraced him and kissed him. His son said to him, "Father, I have sinned against heaven and you, and am not worthy of being called your son..." But his father said to the slaves, "Quick! Bring the finest robe in the house and put it on him. And a jeweled ring for his finger; and shoes! And kill the calf we have in the fattening pen. We must celebrate with a feast, for this son of mine was dead and has returned to life. He was lost and is found." So the party began.

Meanwhile, the older son was in the fields working; when he returned home, he heard dance music coming from the house, and he asked one of the servants what was going on. "Your brother is back," he was told, "and your father has killed the calf we were fattening and has prepared a great feast to celebrate his coming home again unharmed." The older brother was angry and wouldn't go in. His father came out and begged him. But he replied, "All these years I've worked hard for you and never once refused to do a single thing you told me to; and in all that time you never gave me even one young goat for a feast with my friends. Yet when this son of yours comes back after spending your money on prostitutes, you celebrate by killing the finest calf we have on the place."

"Look, dear son," his father said to him, "you and I are very close, and everything I have is yours. But it is right to celebrate. For he is your brother; and he was dead and has come back to life! He was lost and is found!" (see Luke 15:11–32, NLT)

This account contains several important understandings that are highly relevant to our day. First, the father did not try to locate his son and drag him home. The boy was apparently old enough to make his own decisions and the father allowed him to determine his course.

Second, the father did not come to his rescue during the financial stresses that followed. He was a wealthy landowner and could have sent his servants to bring him comfort. Nor did the father send money. There were no well-meaning church groups or governmental agencies that helped support his folly. Note in verses 16 and 17, "No one gave him anything…he finally came to his senses." There is a powerful connection between those verses. The Prodigal Son learned from adversity. The parent who is too anxious to ease the misery of a son or daughter when they have behaved foolishly might be performing a disservice.

Third, the father welcomed his son home without belittling him or demanding reparations. He didn't say, "I told you you'd make a mess of things!" or, "You've embarrassed your mom and me and the whole family. Instead, he ran to meet his son and threw his arms around him. Again, this is the "loving" part of Love Must Be Tough. The father said, "He was lost and is found!" and the family celebrated with a feast. As for the elder brother, he knew how to be tough, but he had no clue about how to love.

Although this understanding of conflict resolution is fairly simple to comprehend, some parents have trouble getting it. If they are afraid to make their child uncomfortable or unhappy when he or she is wrong or sinful (or both), they have to be strong. If the parents lack the determination to win the inevitable confrontations that arise, the child will sense their tentativeness and push them further away. If appeasement occurs, it is curtains for the relationship. The end result will be frustrated, irritated, and ineffectual parents and rebellious, selfish, and even more willful children.

I believe God gave Windsor the wisdom she asked for when her son was on the edge. Meanwhile, the Lord was working on his heart, too. The outcome was remarkable. Zach is doing great. He made a comment recently about the story you just read. He said, "You know, Mom, this is not about me. It is about the faithfulness of God." Amen! As I write, Zach worked last summer at a Christian camp for children and teens. Who knows what the Lord has in store for him?

The program we aired[5] with Mitch and Windsor Yellen has brought a wonderful response to the broadcast and to our website. Windsor is a very effective speaker. If you would like to have her tell her story at a Christian event, you can get information by contacting her assistant, Stephanie, at stephanie@ thepinery.com, or by calling her at 719-475-2600.[6]

CHAPTER NINE

Reaching Our Unsaved Parents

It is often very difficult for sons and daughters to lead their non-believing parents to Jesus Christ. There are many reasons for it, including a reluctance to embarrass or irritate older members of the family. They often assume that spiritual commitments were made at an earlier time, and they ignore the matter. Talking about spiritual concerns is simply too awkward. Our parents brought us into the world and then raised us for eighteen or twenty years. They represented authority, which we either accepted or resisted. Either way, that makes us uneasy when talking about certain issues. Religion can be one of them, unless the generations have similar views. Therefore, convincing Mom or Dad, or brothers and sisters, or uncles and aunts, that they need to repent and accept the claims of Christ is challenging. Typically, the issue is ignored and the years roll by in silence. That isn't always true, but it often is.

Perhaps the experience of our family will be helpful, although none of the aforementioned explanations are relevant to us. Shirley's biological father was an alcoholic and he made about every mistake a man can make. The marriage ended in divorce and Shirley's mom had to work in a fish cannery to keep their little family fed. It was a very difficult era. Shirley's mom knew that she needed help in raising two children, so she sent Shirley and her brother, John, to a little evangelical church, where at six years of age, both of them knelt at an altar and gave their hearts to the Lord. Shirley learned to pray in her little bedroom at night. At twelve years of age when their family was in chaos, she began asking Jesus to grant two requests.

First, Shirley prayed that the Heavenly Father would send her a godly husband when it came time to marry. Though I didn't meet her until we were in college, she was actually praying for me. Second, she asked that the Lord would bring another father to love and care for them. One year later the Lord sent an angel named Joe Kubishta to be Shirley's stepdad. He was thirty-seven years old and had never been married. He was a wonderfully kind and loving man. Given his background, there is no way to account for the "goodness" that lay within him.

Joe was born on a dirt-poor farm near Dickinson, North Dakota, on March 12, 1912. His mother died tragically of tuberculosis when he was nine. She left twelve children, including a baby and a toddler, to fend for themselves. Joe's father was abusive at times and often disappeared for days on drinking binges. The children were forced to drop out of school when Joe was in the eighth grade to work in a coal mine. That was the end of his formal education. He and his siblings were deprived of everything, from parental love to the necessities of life.

Joe left the farm at eighteen years of age when the nation was caught in the grip of the Great Depression. Jobs were scarce, and a young man such as Joe with no money and no influential friends was fortunate to even earn enough to eat. He said, "I never missed a meal during that time but I postponed a few of them." Joe migrated to California, riding the rails, as did many other refugees from Midwestern farms. They were each chasing the promise of work. For the next few years, Joe set pins in a bowling alley, worked on a potato farm, and did whatever was necessary to survive.

How could a man with so many disadvantages and liabilities turn out to be one of the most optimistic, loving, happy, and productive people on earth? I don't know, but I never heard him say a mean thing about another human being. He was known everywhere by his broad grin and by the warmth of his winsome personality. Those who knew Joe Kubishta instantly liked him. I met him many years later when I started dating Shirley, and I came to love him like the father I had lost. We all miss him dearly today.

In 1942, Joe joined the United States Navy and served aboard the battleship *South Dakota*. He fought at Guadalcanal, the Marianas, and Okinawa, among other horrific campaigns in the Pacific. His combat assignment toward the end of the war was to fire a machine gun at deadly Japanese kamikaze planes diving toward the ship. During one terrible battle, a shell exploded on deck, killing 160 men and wounding many others. Thankfully, Joe was not injured. He received numerous medals, including the Navy Unit Commendation for Outstanding Heroism for bravery in the Battle of Guadalcanal. He was honorably discharged on November 3, 1945. Joe was a member of what former NBC news anchor Tom Brokaw termed "The Greatest Generation."[1] They were forged in the fire of privation and discipline, and were intensely patriotic, courageous, and self-sacrificial.

Shortly after the war, Joe met and fell in love with a beautiful woman named Alma Wisham Deere, who had two children, John and Shirley. The Kubishtas were married December 16, 1950, and celebrated their fifty-second anniversary on December 16, 2002. The love and commitment of Joe and Alma to one another are legendary. Joe also loved John and Shirley as though they were his biological children, and he provided stability for them throughout their adolescent years. He became a highly skilled ceramic tile setter and provided admirably for his family until his retirement in 1978, having helped the kids through college. In his years setting tile, he never once had anyone call him back to repair something he had done wrong.

In 1960, I married Shirley Deere and became part of the Kubishta family. Knowing Joe was a highlight of my life. In fact, I referred to my in-laws in my book, *Bringing Up Boys*. This is what I wrote:

I find that children and young people are starved today for family life as it used to be—but almost never is. My in-laws, Joe and Alma Kubishta, are 89 and 90 years of age, and yet my daughter and her friends love to visit their home. Why? Because everything there is so much fun. They have time to play table games, laugh, eat and talk about whatever interests young people. Nobody is in a hurry. If their friends ever called on the phone, they are always available to talk. One of their frequent visitors was an unmarried man named Charlie who just loved the Kubishtas. When he made a return visit to California after moving away, he drove 60 miles to their house with a rosebush that he planted in their backyard. He just wanted to make sure Joe and Alma didn't forget him. [His gift is called "The Charlie Bush" today.] This elderly man and woman provided something to those who are younger that is simply not available elsewhere. How sad.[2]

Here's another quote from my book, written before Joe or Alma died:

This competitive impulse is evident in "boys" of all ages. My father-in-law is getting old, but still loves the thrill of victory. Joe plays golf four to five times per week and keeps track of his wins and losses against his younger buddies. He speaks in a North Dakota accent much like Lawrence Welk, and he loves to tell me this story:

"Hey Jimmy, dos guys I play with, der years younger dan me, and they have coaches to teach them to play golf. But I beat em all. HaHaHaHa."

One of his buddies was named Wally, and Joe would say, "Dat Wally, he practices all week long and he coms out der all set to tak me down, and I beat de socks off him." HaHaHa. Then he always added, "And Wally is ten years younger dan me."

Joesy told me that story until he was ninety years old. He was also very good at a card game called Hearts, which he played during off hours in the Navy. He introduced me to the game when Shirley and I were first married, and Joe played it every time we were together. I had a Ph.D. and Joe never went to high school, but he beat "de socks off me," too. It took me three years to figure out how Joe was whipping me. He offered no hints. He just laughed and said, "Let's play again." I finally cracked the code. When Joe had a good hand and was quietly trying to "run it," his blood pressure went up and his neck turned red. I used to watch that region below his ears and I could tell what he was thinking. You see, Joe wasn't the only one who "loved to win." But he still usually beat me.

Joe was incredibly healthy until the very end of his life. He had had one small dental cavity in ninety years, and was in the hospital only once for something relatively minor. He continued playing golf regularly until six months before his death. Believe it or not, Joe shot an eighty-seven on his ninetieth birthday, and made a "hole in one" when he was eighty-five. A photo taken as Joe retrieved his ball after that miraculous drive appears in the photo section of this book.

Now I must tell you about Joe's spiritual life. I don't think he was a Christian when he married Alma. At least if he was, he never talked about it. He came out of an era when people didn't like to discuss their faith, and he considered his convictions to be a very personal matter. As the years passed, our family talked often about Jesus Christ, and even then he was reluctant to let us in on this private world. Nevertheless, when Alma was sick for any reason, Joe would get dressed on Sunday morning and go to a nearby Baptist church. We prayed before every meal, and Joe would sometimes lead, but still, he never said the words we wanted to hear.

Finally, I took him to lunch one day, just the two of us, and I said, "Joe, I really need to talk to you about something important. You know that we can't be together in heaven unless you have a personal relationship with Jesus Christ. I think I know the answer, but you have never told me how you became a Christian. Share that story with me."

Joe said, "Oh, Jimmy, you don hav to worry bout dat. When I was nine years old (which meant when his mother died) a priest took me into a little room and he talk to me."

Frankly, I didn't know what that meant and it stymied me. I couldn't say, "Oh, no, Joe, that didn't count. You haven't been a Christian all these years." He acted like he knew the Lord personally, but he never came out and said it. I just wasn't sure if he fully understood what a relationship with Christ meant. I did the best I could to explain it, but he just smiled.

When we were told a year later by a hematologist that Joe was dying of leukemia, Shirley and I felt a great urgency to assure that he was ready to meet his Maker. The stakes were too high to leave anything to speculation. I came to his bedside in the hospital and said, "Joe, do you know for certain that you will be with us in heaven when you die?" He promptly changed the subject. Then I said rather sternly, "Joe, look at me. I asked you a question and I want you to answer it." There was no time to waste. With that, he turned his face to the wall and wept. None of us had ever seen Joe cry before. He was, for the first time, very tender to the gentle touch of the Spirit.

The next day, Shirley called Joe's minister at his Baptist church and asked him to come and talk to him. Rev. Lyle Williams sat at his bedside and said, "You know, I have been preaching a series of sermons on hope, especially our hope of eternal life." They talked a while and then the minister skillfully led Joe in the sinner's prayer. Then, a marvelous thing happened. Joe asked Jesus to come into his heart. No doubt about it. The next day when Shirley and I visited, he was beaming. He held his hands in the air and said with tears streaming down his face, "JIMMY, I'M SAVED. I'M SAVED!" This came from a man who had never been willing to talk about his faith. I knelt beside him and said, "Joe, every sin that you have committed in your entire life has been forgiven, and they will never be remembered against you again. We're going to be together in heaven forever and ever." Shirley and I were both crying.

The next day when we arrived at the hospital, Joe began crying again. "I'm clean," he said. "I feel so clean." It was a wonderful experience to see this precious soul, who may or may not have been justified earlier in the eyes of God, make a public confession of his dedication to his Lord and Savior, Jesus Christ. He experienced what we in our faith community call "a conversion."

Though Joe was indeed dying that November, we asked God for one more Thanksgiving and one more Christmas together, and unbelievably, he was able to come home from the hospital on both days. He sat at a window looking out at the Pacific Ocean for a long time without talking. I think he was saying "good-bye." Then he said, "Okay, Jimmy, I want to go back to de hospital." We were given ten more weeks with the man Shirley lovingly called "Pops," and our kids called him "Grandpa Joe," and I called him "Joesy."

Even as he approached the end, everyone at the medical facility had fallen in love with Joe. One of his nurses said to Shirley, "I just love that man. All he talks about is how much he loves his wife. I wish I could put him in my pocket and take him home."

His doctor, a crusty older Jewish physician, said to me in the hall one afternoon, "Everyone loves that man in there," pointing to Joe's room. "You wanna know why? 'Cause he's a good man. He's never had much money, but he worked hard all his life. He's the kind of man who built this country."

Toward the end, I asked Joe if he was comfortable and if the hospital staff was treating him well. He said, "Oh, Jimmy, der good to me here. Dis is a great place. Da food is good. I couldn't ask for anything better." As he spoke, I thought about this emaciated human being, lying on his bed all day with nothing to do but stare at the walls. Yet there was not a hint of self-pity in his demeanor. A Scripture verse came to my mind as he lay on his deathbed. The Apostle Paul had written it when he was in a Philippian prison and would soon be executed. Who knows what miserable circumstances he was encountering, and yet this is what he wrote:

> I have learned the secret of being content in any and every situation, whether well fed or hungry, whether living in plenty or in want. I can do everything through him who gives me strength. (Phil. 4:12–13)

Joe Kubishta exemplified this peace and contentment as well as anyone I've ever known.

On February 14, Valentine's Day, Joe was voted "King of Hearts" by the medical staff and the patients at the convalescent hospital. He had trouble stringing words together coherently by that point, but it didn't matter. His winning personality was still evident. We played one last game of Hearts, and he couldn't remember the rules. How sad that was. Four days later, on February 18, he told Shirley that the angels were coming to get him. And on February 19, my beloved father-in-law slipped quietly out of this life and into eternity. He was nearly ninety-one years old. Now he awaits the rest of our family on the other side. I promise you, Joe will be smiling!

I'll share one last story that was related during the memorial service. Our son Ryan, who has become a very effective speaker, gave one of the emotional eulogies. During his remarks he talked about the meaning of success. Ryan described a day several months earlier when he dropped by unexpectedly at his grandparents' house. He found them sitting at the kitchen table—not on opposite sides, but side by side. They were holding hands.

"What are you doing?" Ryan asked.

"We've just been sitting here this morning looking at one another," Alma replied.

After fifty-two years of marriage, they were content just to be in each other's company. "THAT," said Ryan, "is my definition of marital success." Joe Kubishta was survived by his wife, Alma, who died six years later, and by his stepson John and John's wife, Marlene Deere; their grown sons, Steve and Brad Deere; by his stepdaughter, Shirley, and me, his son-in-law; and by our grown children, Danae and Ryan Dobson. As soon as I have been in heaven for a while and have knelt at the feet of Jesus, I want to play a game of Hearts with Joe. I know he will win.

Good-bye, our beloved husband, father, grandfather, and friend. You brought such incredible joy into our lives. Your smile and laughter will linger in our memories forever. We can hardly imagine life without you, but our separation will be brief. We will see you on the other side, in the presence of our wonderful Lord and Savior, Jesus Christ. Because He lives, we can face tomorrow.

Neither height nor depth, nor anything else in all creation, will be able to separate us from the love of God that is in Christ Jesus our Lord. (Rom. 8:39)

—◦◦◦—

I have one more story to tell you about the salvation of a loved one. I believe it will resonate with you as you think about your own kin. This one is about my father's father, my grandfather, Robert Lee Dobson. He is legendary in the Dobson family.

My grandfather never professed to be a Christian. It's the old story about seeing hypocrites in the church and wanting nothing to do with them. He never opposed Little Mother's spiritual training of their six children, including riding a streetcar across Shreveport to get them in church. She was a member of the board there. Grandfather Dobson had no objection to his wife doing that. He even let her support the church with contributions. However, he steadfastly refused any involvement of his own.

"Keep me out of it," he said. "I want nothing to do with Christianity or any church."

My grandmother was deeply troubled by her husband's rejection of spiritual matters. He was a "moral" man but that is as far as it went. Little Mother didn't press him about his faith, but she made it a lifelong project to pray for her husband. For forty years she continued this quiet prayer vigil without any movement on his part.

When Robert was sixty-eight, he suffered a massive stroke and was bedridden thereafter. The following year, his youngest child, a teenager named Elizabeth, was in his room taking care of him and giving him his medications. She then looked toward his bed and saw that he was crying. That was most unusual for this stoic man.

Elizabeth said, "Daddy, what's wrong?"

He replied barely above a whisper, "Honey, go get your mother."

My grandmother ran up the stairs in the Big House and knelt at her husband's bedside. She said, "Are you okay?"

Robert said to her, "I know now that I am going to die and I am not afraid of death. But it is *so* dark. Will you pray for me?"

"Will I pray?" she asked through her tears.

Little Mother had been praying for this moment for four decades. She began to pray for the man she loved, and he surrendered his heart to the Lord. I wish I could have been there on that occasion. R. L. Dobson died two weeks later with a testimony on his lips.

At Christmastime thirty-five years later, four surviving siblings came to my parents' home in California for their first family reunion since the death of their father. For five days they sat in the living room and shared treasured memories from their childhood. Almost all of their conversations centered on their dad, although Little Mother and their twin brothers were gone by that time, too. I was enthralled by what I heard. One of my cousins recorded their recollections on a small cassette tape machine and they still exist today. What a rich heritage these recordings provide, granting insight into my grandparents' home and the early experiences of my dad and his siblings.

While all the conversations were of interest to me, there was a common thread that was especially significant throughout the week. It focused on the respect with which these four siblings addressed the memory of their father (my grandfather). He died in 1935, a year before my birth, yet they spoke of him with an unmistakable awe more than thirty-four years later. He still lived in their minds as a man of enormous character and strength.

I asked them to explain the qualities that they admired so greatly, but received little more than vague generalities.

"He was a tower of strength," said one.

"He had a certain dignity about him," said another, with appropriate gestures.

"We held him in awe," replied the third.

It is difficult to summarize the subtleties and complexities of the human personality, and they were unable to find the right words. Only when they began talking about specific memories did the personality of this patriarch become apparent. My dad provided the best evidence by writing his recollection of Grandfather Dobson's death, which I've reproduced below. Flowing throughout this narrative is the impact of a great man on his family, even three decades after his demise. This is my dad's written account.

The Last Days of R. L. Dobson

The attack that took his life occurred when he was sixty-nine years of age, and resulted ultimately in the breakup of the family circle. For many years after his death, I could not pass Tri-State Hospital in Shreveport without noting one particular window. It stood out from the rest, hallowed because it represented the room where he had suffered so much. The details of those tragic days and nights remain in my memory, unchanged by the passage of time.

We had been three days and three nights practically without sleep, listening to him struggle for breath, hearing the sounds of approaching death, smelling the smells of death. Dad lay in a deep coma. His heavy breathing could be heard up and down the corridor. We walked the halls of that old hospital for hours listening to the ceaseless struggle which now was becoming fainter and fainter. Several times the nurse had called us in and we had said the last "goodbye"—had gone through the agony of giving him up, only to have his heart rally, and then the endless vigil would begin all over again. Finally, we had gone into an adjoining room not prepared for sleep, but some in the chairs and some across the beds, we had fallen into the sleep of utter exhaustion.

At five minutes to four o'clock the nurse came in and awakened one of my twin brothers. Robert roused with a start. "Is he gone?" he asked.

"No, but if you boys want to see your dad one more time while he is alive, you'd better come, now."

The word quickly passed around and we filed into the room to stand around his bed for the last time. I remember that I stood at his left side: I smoothed back the hair from his forehead, and laid my hand on his big old red hand, so very much like my own. I felt the fever that precedes death: 105. While I was standing there a change came over me. Instead of being a grown man (I was twenty-four at the time) I became a little boy again. They say this often happens to adults who witness the death of a parent. I thought I was in the Union Train Station in Shreveport, Louisiana, in the late afternoon, and I was watching for his return. The old Kansas City Southern passenger train was backing into the station and I saw it come 'round the curve. My heart swelled with pride. I turned to the little boy standing next to me and said, "You see that big man standing on the back of the train, one hand on the air brake and the other on the little whistle with which he signals the engineer? That big man is my dad!" He set the air brakes and I heard the wheels grind to a stop. I saw him step off that last coach. I ran and jumped into his arms. I gave him a tight hug and I smelled the train smoke on his clothes. "Daddy, I love you," I said.

It all comes back. I patted that big hand and said "Goodbye, Dad," as he was sinking fast, now. "We haven't forgotten how hard you worked to send five boys and one girl through college: how you wore those old conductor uniforms until they were slick—doing without—that we might have things that we didn't really need..."

At three minutes to four o'clock, like a stately ship moving slowly out of time's harbor into eternity's sea, he breathed his last. The nurse motioned for us to leave, and pulled the sheet over his head, a gesture that struck terror to my heart. We turned with silent weeping to leave the room. Then an incident occurred that I will never forget. Just as we got to the door, I put my arm around my little mother and said, "Mama, this is awful."

Dabbing at her eyes with her handkerchief, she said, "Yes, Jimmy, but there is one thing Mother wants you to remember, now. We have said 'good night' down here, but one of these days we are going to say 'good morning' up there." I believe she did say "good morning" too, eleven years later, and I know he met her "just inside the Eastern gate."

His death was marked by quietness and dignity, just like the life he had lived. Thus came to an end the affairs of R. L. Dobson, and it ended, too, the solidarity of the family. The old home place was never the same again. The old spirit that we had known as children was gone forever!

Though this illustration reveals few of the specific characteristics that made R. L. Dobson such a powerful influence in his family, it does tell us how his son felt about him. I happen to know some of the other details. He was a man of absolute integrity and honesty. Though not a Christian until shortly before his death, he lived by an internal standard that was singularly uncompromising. As a young man, for example, he invested heavily in a business venture with a partner whom he later discovered to be dishonest. When he learned of the chicanery, he virtually gave the company to the other man. That former partner built the corporation into one of the most successful operations in the South, and he became a multimillionaire. But my grandfather never regretted his decision. He took a clean conscience with him to his grave.

How about your family? Are there members who are not safely within the fold of the faith? If so, may I urge you to intensify your prayers on their behalf, and watch patiently for an opportunity to tell them again about finding a relationship with Jesus? It might be, as in the case of Joe Kubishta and Robert Lee Dobson, that time and circumstances will open a door that has previously been closed. We can't make a person willing to repent of sins and accept divine forgiveness, but if that occurs even to the point of death, the angels in heaven will rejoice. And you and your other believing family members will live out your years knowing that a joyous reunion is in store on what Little Mother anticipated as a "good morning, just inside the Eastern Gate."

Dr. Dobson's maternal great-grandfather, Rev. George Washington McCluskey.

George W. and Alice ("Nanny") McCluskey.

Dr. Dobson's maternal grandparents, Rev. Michael Vance and Bessie Dillingham, known to the family as "Little Daddy and Big Mama."

Early photo of the Dillingham family. James Dobson Sr. stands at the left. Myrtle Dobson, seated at left, holds four-year-old son Jimmy. At the right, seated, is Myrtle's sister Lela London, holding her son, H.B. His father, Holland London, is standing in the back row, third from the right.

James Dobson Sr. and Myrtle Dobson with their baby son, Jimmy.

Myrtle and her much-loved little boy.

James and Myrtle with their kindergartner, Jimmy.

The first church
pastored by
Reverend Dobson
in Sulphur Springs,
Texas, 1937.

Alma Kubishta and her four-year-old
daughter, Shirley.

Shirley and her brother,
John, at ages eight and ten.

Classic photo of Dad, his son, and their beloved dog, Penny, during Jim's college days, 1958. In the background is the house in which Jim grew up. He had just come home for Christmas.

Jim and cousin H.B. London, as college roommates. Can you tell they were rivals?

Jim's college graduation photo, 1958.

Jim in his U.S. Army fatigues in 1959.

Shirley's homecoming queen photo, 1959.

Myrtle Dobson in Hawaii, 1956.

Last photo of Rev. James Dobson Sr., taken just before his death in 1977.

Dr. Dobson's parents in 1960.

Photos taken of Jimmy as a teen, and Jim caught in the same pensive mood more than fifty-five years later. (*Right side credit: Harry Langdon*)

Another then-and-now setting, featurin Jim and Shirley in a wedding photo, and a similar pose taken in their fiftieth anniversary year. (*Right side credit: Greg Schneider*)

Wedding night for Jim and Shirley, with her parents, Joe and Alma Kubishta, and his parents, James and Myrtle Dobson. The date was August 27, 1960.

Jim graduating and receiving his Ph.D. in child development at USC seven years later. Does he look tired? Hint: Yes.

Joe Kubishta retrieving his ball after shooting a hole-in-one at eighty-seven years of age.

Proud parents show off
their baby, Danae Ann,
on Dedication Sunday.

Shirley and four-year-old
Danae wearing hot pink. It
was Easter Sunday morning.

James Ryan joins
the Dobson
family in 1970.

Danae and her little
brother, Ryan, huddle
together in the front yard
of their home. She was five
and he was six months old.

Danae and Ryan at his high school graduation.

Ryan and Jim in a radio studio, talking about *Bringing Up Boys*.

Ryan and his dad began hunting together when he was twelve. Here they are pictured on a pheasant hunt. They both treasure those times.

Father and daughter.

This portrait of Danae hangs in her dad's office. (*Credit: Greg Schneider*)

Shirley and her mother. Alma was eighty-four and lived to be ninety-seven.

A recent family portrait featuring Ryan and his wife, Laura, at left, and their two-year-old son, Lincoln. (*Credit: Harry Langdon*)

"Jimpa" and "Mae Mae" with two-year-old Lincoln. (*Credit: Laura Dobson*)

And along came Luci, shown here at two years of age. (*Credit: Laura Dobson*)

James Dobson interviewing President Ronald Reagan on radio in the Oval Office. The year was 1987.

Dr. Dobson interviewing President George H. W. Bush at Focus on the Family in 1992. Note the book they were discussing.

The Dobsons attend a Christmas celebration at the White House with President George W. Bush and Laura.

Shirley entering the East Room of the White House to speak during a National Day of Prayer event. Note who is trailing along behind. (*Credit: AP photo/Pablo Martinez Monsivais*)

Shirley Dobson presents a bound copy of forty-nine proclamations from the nation's governors to President George W. Bush during the May 2001 National Day of Prayer.

A moment of solemn prayer for the nation during the ceremony. President Bush held National Day of Prayer events every year through his two terms in office. Shirley spoke at all eight, from 2001 to 2009. (*Credit: AP photo/Ron Edwards*)

A private meeting at the invitation of His Royal Highness, the Prince of Wales, Prince Charles, at his estate, Highgrove, in the Cotswolds. Their conversation is confidential.

The Dobsons with Pope John Paul II. Dr. Dobson and Chuck Colson had just spoken at an International Pontificate on the Family. They are the first two evangelicals to speak at the historic Synod Building in the Vatican. (*Credit: www .fotografiafelici.com, Rome, Italy*)

Dr. Dobson and Dr. Billy Graham converse before a crusade event.

Dr. Dobson was asked to carry the Olympic torch for a short distance in the lead-up to the Winter Games in Salt Lake City, 2002. (*Credit: Colorado Springs Gazette/Carol Lawrence*)

Dobson and Focus on the Family are inducted into the National Radio Hall of Fame in 2008. Other designees are Ronald Reagan, Jack Benny, Bob Hope, Red Skelton, Larry King, Rush Limbaugh, Paul Harvey, Franklin D. Roosevelt, and many others. (*Credit: Donald Pointer Photography*)

Jim and Shirley cut the cake during the celebration of their fiftieth wedding anniversary in 2010. Danae and Ryan hosted the event.(*Credit: Kevin Still*)

Jim is a great cook. Here he is frying chicken using a recipe taught to him by his mother. Those who have been treated to this Southern dish say it is scrumptious. (*Credit: Julie Johnson*)

This photo of Shirley's Easter table was chosen to be the cover of Shirley and Danae's book, *Welcome to Our Table*. (*Credit: Julie Johnson*)

Jim is the author of forty books. Here he is writing, writing, writing. (*Credit: Beau Henderson*)

Dr. Dobson with a bronze depiction of his father in prayer, which was sculpted by Greg Todd.

CHAPTER TEN

Words Matter

I stated earlier that the culture is at war with parents for the hearts and minds of their children. I don't need to describe this battle because you see it, too. Parents in decades past would not have believed what was about to happen to the institution of the family. I am not sure many of us understand it, either. Immorality, pornography, violence, and illicit drugs touch almost every home. Most moms and dads love their children and are trying to shepherd them past the minefields that lie scattered in their paths. However, they are perplexed by the challenges they face.

When I was a kid, parental authority typically stood like a great shield against the evils in what was called "the world." Anything perceived as unwholesome or immoral was kept outside the white picket fence simply by willing it to stay put. Furthermore, the surrounding community was helpful to families.

It was organized to keep kids on the straight and narrow. Censorship prevented the movies from going too far, schools maintained strict discipline, disrespectful or rebellious students were "paddled" or found themselves sitting in "detention," infractions were reported to the parents, truant officers caught students playing hooky, chaperones usually preserved virginity, alcohol was not sold to minors, and illicit drugs were unheard-of. Even unrelated adults saw it as their civic responsibility to help protect children from anything that could harm them, whether physically, emotionally, or spiritually. Most townsfolk were acquainted with other children's parents, so it was easier for them to intervene. This support system didn't always do the job, of course, but it was generally effective.

This commitment to the welfare of children has all but vanished. Rather than assisting parents in their child-rearing responsibilities, the pop culture and politically correct ideology conspires against them. The Judeo-Christian system of values is on the wane. Harmful images and ideas come sliding under the front door or they slither directly into the bedrooms through electronic media. Illicit drugs are available to every teen or preteen who wants them. Everything changes for those who are taking them. With every child having a cell phone with which to access each other beyond parental ears, and with the advent of the all-pervasive social media, there are just too many opportunities for kids to conspire and to get into trouble. Controlling those ever-changing dynamics of child development puts our kids at greater risk and their parents in disarray.

Considering how the world has changed, it is no longer enough to make and enforce rules to keep children in line. It still makes sense to prohibit harmful or immoral behavior, and to discipline and punish when appropriate. However, these time-honored approaches to child management must be supplemented by an emotional connection that makes children *want* to do what is right. In short, it is doubly important to build relationships with kids from their earliest childhood. Your sons and daughters must know that you love them unconditionally and that everything you require is for their own good. It is also helpful to explain why you want them to behave in certain ways. "Laying down the law" without this emotional linkage is likely to fail.

Author and speaker Josh McDowell expressed this principle in a single sentence. He said, "Rules without relationship lead to rebellion."[1] He is absolutely right. With all the temptations buzzing around our kids, simply saying no a thousand times creates a spirit of defiance. We have to build bridges to them from the ground up. The construction should begin early and include having fun as a family, laughing and joking, playing board games, throwing or kicking a ball, shooting baskets, playing Ping-Pong, running with the dog, talking at bedtime, swimming together, participating in sports, getting kids in great churches with good youth programs, being a sponsor of the school band, and doing a thousand other things that tend to cement the generations together. The tricky part is to establish friendships while maintaining parental authority and respect. It can be done. It must be done. It is the only formula I know to combat the dangers that stalk the land. But it takes time—about which my dad said, "cannot be given if it is all signed and conscripted and laid on the altar of career ambition."

Ryan and I hunted and fished together, which bonded us together like Gorilla Glue. It still holds today. Shirley did girly things with Danae throughout childhood. She and I played volleyball and Ping-Pong and croquet in the backyard. Our home had an open door. Our children's friends were welcome, and some of them almost lived with us. There was always a buzz of activity during the teen years. We fed them pizza and played games and watched clean movies. As the kids got older, we budgeted money to make skiing our centerpiece. That was the most wonderful decision we made. After a full day on the slopes with friends from both generations, we ate a good dinner and then engaged each other in meaningful devotions and Bible studies. These experiences were almost always interesting and lasted up to two hours per night. At dawn the next morning, we were back on the ski lifts and headed to the summit for another great day. This is how we got our kids through the challenges of adolescence. Shirley broke her leg on the slopes at Vail, Colorado, but she suffered gracefully, knowing that raising good kids always requires a few sacrifices.

I know not every family can afford to ski when children are growing up, but building relationships doesn't necessarily require large amounts of money. A lifelong connection often emerges from simple traditions that give meaning and identity to families. Children love daily routines and activities of the simplest kind. They want to hear the same story or the same joke until Mom and Dad are ready to climb the wall. And yet, these interactions are sometimes more appreciated by kids than are expensive toys or special events.

Beloved author and professor, the late Dr. Howard Hendricks, once asked his grown children what they remembered most fondly from their childhood. Was it the vacations they took or the trips to theme parks or the zoo? "No," they answered. It was when Dad got on the floor and wrestled with them.[2] That's the way children think. It is especially the way boys think. The most meaningful activities in a family are often those simple interactions that build lasting connections between generations.

Let's describe what we mean by traditions. They refer to repetitive activities that give identity and belonging to every member of the family. In the Broadway musical *Fiddler on the Roof*, the fiddler was perched securely on top of the house because of tradition. These historical customs, dictated to every member of the Jewish community who he or she was and how to deal with the demands of life and even what to wear or eat. There is comfort and security for children when they know what is expected and how they fit into the scheme of things.

Two friends, Greg Johnson and Mike Yorkey, offered some examples of how *not* to build good relationships with your kids in their book *Daddy's Home*. These suggestions were written with tongue in cheek, but I think they got their point across.

Have the NBA game of the week on while you're playing Monopoly with them.

Read the paper while helping them with their algebra assignments.

Go to the local high school football field to practice your golf swing and have your kids collect the balls after you're done.

Suggest they take a nap with you on a beautiful Sunday afternoon.

Drive them to Cub Scouts and read a magazine in the car while the den mother instructs them on how to tie knots.

Take them to your office on Saturday and have them color while you work.[3]

Clearly, there are many ways to fake it—appearing to care and "be involved" when you're actually just babysitting. I guarantee you, however, that your kids won't be fooled for long. They can see through adult pretenses with something akin to X-ray vision. And they will remember that you were or were not there for them when they were reaching for you. Someone said, "Love is giving somebody your undivided attention." It is a great definition.

Here's another idea relevant to relationships that I think makes a lot of sense. It's called "the first five minutes" and is based on a book that was published many years ago. Its thesis was that the first five minutes occurring between people sets the tone for everything that is to follow. For example, a public speaker is given very few moments to convince his audience that he really does have something worthwhile to say. If he's boring or stilted in the beginning, his listeners will turn him off like a lightbulb and he'll never know why. And if he hopes to use humor during his speech, he'd better say something funny very quickly or they won't believe he can make them laugh. The opportunity of the moment is lost. Fortunately, whenever we begin a new interaction, we have a chance to reset the mood.

This simple principle relates to family members as well. The first five minutes of the morning also determine how a mother will interact with her children on that day. Snarls or complaints as the kids gather for breakfast will sour their relationship for hours. Greeting children after school with kind words and a tasty snack may be remembered for decades. And at the end of the day when a man arrives home from work, the way he greets his wife, or doesn't greet his wife, will influence their interaction throughout the evening. A single criticism such as, "Not tuna casserole again!" will put their relationship on edge from then to bedtime. Men who complain that their wives are not affectionate at bedtime should think back to the first moments when they came together in the evening. He probably messed up some great possibilities with his first snippy comments.

It all starts with the first five minutes.

While we are talking about relationships, there is another issue we should discuss. It concerns the sheer power of words. They are so easy to utter, often tumbling out without much reason or forethought. Those who hurl criticism or hostility at others may not even mean or believe what they have said. Their comments may reflect momentary jealousy, resentment, depression, fatigue, or revenge. Regardless of the intent, harsh words sting like killer bees. Almost all of us, including you and me, have lived through moments when a parent, a teacher, a friend, a colleague, a husband, or a wife said something that cut to the quick. That hurt is now sealed forever in the memory bank. That is an amazing property of the spoken word. Even though a person forgets most of his or her day-by-day experiences, a particularly painful comment may be remembered for decades. By contrast, the individual who did the damage may have no memory of the encounter a few days later.

Former first lady Hillary Rodham Clinton told a story about her father, who never affirmed her as a child. When she was in high school, she brought home a straight-A report card. She showed it to her dad, hoping for a word of commendation. Instead, he said, "Well, you must be attending an easy school." All these years later the remark still burns in Mrs. Clinton's mind. His thoughtless response may have represented nothing more than a casual quip, but it created a point of pain that has endured to this day.[4]

There is wisdom about the impact of words written in the book of James. The passage reads,

When we put bits into the mouths of horses to make them obey us, we can turn the whole animal. Or take ships as an example. Although they are so large and are driven by strong winds, they are steered by a very small rudder wherever the pilot wants to go. Likewise the tongue is a small part of the body, but it makes great boasts. Consider what a great forest is set on fire by a small spark. The tongue also is a fire, a world of evil among the parts of the body. It corrupts the whole person, sets the whole course of his life on fire, and is itself set on fire by hell. (James 3:3–6)

Have you ever set yourself or others on fire with sparks spraying from your tongue? More important, have you ever set a child's spirit on fire with anger? All of us have made that costly mistake. We knew we had blundered the moment the comment flew out of our mouths, but it was too late. If we tried for a hundred years, we couldn't take back a single remark. The first year Shirley and I were married, she became very angry with me about something that neither of us can recall. In the frustration of the moment she said, "If this is marriage, I don't want any part of it." She didn't mean it and regretted her words almost immediately. An hour later we had reconciled and forgiven each other, but Shirley's statement could not be taken back. We've laughed about it through the years and the issue is inconsequential today. Still, there is nothing either of us can do to erase the utterance of the moment.

Words are not only remembered for a lifetime, but if not

forgiven, they endure beyond the chilly waters of death. We read in Matthew 12:36,

> But I tell you that everyone will have to give account on the day of judgment for every empty word they have spoken.

Thank God, those of us who have a personal relationship with Jesus Christ are promised that our sins—and our harsh words—will be remembered against us no more and will be removed "as far as the east is from the west" (Ps. 103:12a). Apart from that atonement, however, our words will follow us forever.

I didn't intend to preach a sermon here, but I find great inspiration for all family relationships within the great wisdom of the Scriptures. And so it is with the impact of what we say. The scary thing for us parents is that we never know when the mental videotape is running during our interactions with children and teens. A spontaneous critical comment that means little to us at the time may "stick" and be repeated long after we are dead and gone. By contrast, the warm and affirming things we say about our sons and daughters may be a source of satisfaction for decades. Again, it is all in the power of words.

The circumstances that precipitate a hurtful comment for a child or teen are irrelevant to their impact. Let me explain. Even though a child pushes you to the limit, frustrating and angering you to the point of exasperation, you will nevertheless pay a price for overreacting. Let's suppose you lose your poise and shout, "I can't stand you! I wish you belonged to someone else." Or, "I can't believe you failed another test. How could a son of mine be so stupid!" Even if every normal parent would also have been agitated in the same situation, your child will not focus on his misbehavior in the future. He is likely to forget what he did to cause your outburst. But he will recall the day that you said you didn't want him or that he was stupid. It isn't fair, but neither is life.

I know I'm stirring a measure of guilt into the mix with these comments. (My words are powerful, too, aren't they?) My purpose, however, is not to hurt you but to make you mindful that everything you say has lasting meaning for a child. He may forgive you later for "setting the fire," but how much better it would have been to have stayed cool. You can learn to do that with prayer and practice.

I've strayed a bit from my theme of relationships, but I think the discussion of words was important. Returning to the issue at hand, the day is coming when those of you with young children will need to draw on the foundation of love and caring that you have built. If resentment and rejection characterized the early years, the adolescent experience might be a nightmare. The best way to avoid this teenage time bomb is to defuse it in childhood. That is done with a healthy balance of authority and love at home. Begin now to build a relationship that will see you through the storms of adolescence.

To summarize, a close-knit family is what keeps boys and girls grounded when the world is enticing them to break loose. In this day, you dare not become disconnected during the time when everything is on the line. If you do the job effectively, it will be easier to introduce your children to Jesus Christ. Remember this: If they know you care, you'll be more effective in teaching them what you believe!

CHAPTER ELEVEN

The Saga of Two Good Men

Recently, I was privileged to hear remarks made by two men who spoke at a National Day of Prayer event in Washington, D.C. Only men were present, and the testimonies we heard touched everyone who attended. I'm going to share their personal stories with you because I believe they will hit near where you live.

We'll hear first from Russ Branzell. He has served in numerous health-care leadership positions, including his present assignment as CEO/President of the College of Healthcare Information Management Executives (CHIME).[1] He also served in the U.S. Air Force for twenty years. He is married to Kathy and they have two children, Chandler (20) and Emily (16).

Then Craig Dance will share his story. He is the owner and president of Champion Coach.[2] He is married to Hazel and they have three children, Matthew (21), Jacob (18), and Anna (16).

Both Kathy and Hazel are deeply committed Christians, and as you will see, they have been influential at critical times in their husbands' spiritual walks. Thus, these two transcripts will have "takeaway value" not only for men but for women, too.

I admire these two families and appreciate them allowing me to invade their private lives.

—⁓—

Comments by Russ Branzell

Good morning. I want to begin my comments today with a verse that will be the basis for what I will share with you. That passage is, "Trust in the Lord with all your heart and lean not on your own understanding" (Prov. 3:5).

My story begins with my answering a call to salvation back in the late seventies. Then there was a long period of apathy from then until 2011. Those were what I call "the dark years." I wasn't living for anything but myself. The reason for my lack of growth was that I had an addiction. I wasn't involved in drugs, alcohol, or sex. I was gripped by something even more addictive than that. Millions of men are afflicted with it, and I was a carrier. Here are some of the symptoms of this disorder. It is the tendency to become overcommitted and driven for success, and the hunger for promotions, and the lust for power, money, and more "stuff." I had a poor relationship with my wife and kids; I had no really good friends. I was in debt, especially from my abuse of credit cards, and I wanted more cars and houses. It was always a desire for more, more, more.

I was depressed almost every day. I was overweight, and consequentially, I was hypertensive. I was also prediabetic, and all my lab tests were out of whack. Generally, I was a miserable human being. You know people like that. They are all around us. Their lifestyle reflects the desire for pleasure of all varieties. I had this addiction for three decades and it controlled me.

Finally in 2011, I'd had enough. Rephrase that. God had had enough. Have you ever had Him tap you on the shoulder and talk straight to you? He sometimes speaks in a whisper, and then in a gentle voice. Occasionally, He hits you with a two-by-four. I can tell you that I have had many bumps on the back of my head. And the question He asked me in 2011 was quite simple. He said, "Do you trust Me? Do you *really* trust Me?" My answer was a little wishy-washy. I said, "Well, I kind of trust You."

Many of you know my wife Kathy. She is committed to Christ like Craig's wife, Hazel, is. We both "married up." The Lord then said to me, "Tell Kathy everything. Come clean. Talk to her about your life. Talk about your stresses. Talk about your fears, your weaknesses. Admit everything your life has come down to." As you would guess if you know Kathy, she said, "Let's attack this together with God's help." She went straight to her knees and began praying for me. Then she said, "What are we going to deal with first on this list?" Then she answered her own question: "Let's attack something tangible, such as our debt."

We began talking about how we dealt with money. We signed up at our church for the Dave Ramsey class and sat in a room with a hundred people. I began to realize that we had as much debt as the rest of the class combined. Literally. When we completed our "Ramsey plan," we saw that if we did everything right, we would be close to debt-free in five to seven years. So with a lot of strength from my wife, much prayer, and the Lord's leading, we said, "Let's do it. Let's just follow the entire program." The very first thing they taught us was to begin tithing.

Okay. Now, wait a second. This doesn't make sense, does it? I'm knee-deep in debt and the first thing I need to do is begin giving money away? The leaders didn't just want me to start tithing. They told me to begin giving above that level. Start giving generously to the Lord. Test Him. Really? You want me to *test* the Lord? Well, that made no sense to me. But we checked it out in the Scriptures. And it was there in the Book of Malachi. It says to "test the Lord." We began there.

In the next four months, two weird business deals that I had made were sold. I didn't even know I had stock in them. Honestly, I didn't. I was on the board for one of these companies and it was about to go under. I expected to never hear from it again. But these two companies sold, and in four months, our debt was gone. It was shocking to us. Every bill was paid! All we owed was the mortgage on our house, which is right in line with the Ramsey plan.

Now I don't care if you believe it or not, but what happened was an amazing "God thing." We were not only out of debt, but we were able to bless various ministries. We were able to help our church. It was very gratifying.

However, by early 2012, as with any powerful addiction, I began falling back into my old habits. So the Lord brought out the two-by-four. Again, He said, "Do you really trust Me?" I had a little more confidence this time, and I said, "Yes, Lord. What do You want of me?"

He said, "I want you to start rebuilding your family. I want you to make new friends. I want you to develop a relationship with your son, your daughter, your wife, and your friends. I want you to build friendships with people you can lean on because this is going to get tougher, not easier."

I said, "Okay, Lord."

Today I have a much better relationship with my family. I have some great friends, and I can pick up the phone or text them and they will be right there for me any time of the night or day. When you're struggling, and when you're tempted, when you just need a friend, they're there. But that was a difficult process. I had to give a lot of myself to get there.

Out came another two-by-four. The Lord said again, "Do you really trust me?"

At that time, I was very fortunate to be invited to a golf tournament called the Payne Stewart Cup. Payne had a wonderful walk of faith near the end of his life, and he and his friends organized a golf tournament in St. Andrews, Scotland. I thought it was just a bunch of guys going to play golf with some cool PGA pros. I had no idea this was a men's ministry. The pros included Wally Armstrong, who has written books on faith, and Bill Rogers, who won the '81 British Open Championship.[3] We played some good golf, but it was actually about one thing. They asked the participants, "Do you have a personal friendship/relationship with Jesus Christ? Is He the person sitting right next to you in everything you do in your life?" To be honest I don't remember the golf. All I remember is I was changed. I came back and said, "I've got to discover who this person is."

My calling was to sanctification, which means becoming like Christ, and to follow Him. There was an overwhelming longing in my soul. And I changed unbelievably. I asked myself, "Can I really have a personal relationship with the God of the universe? Can He be *my* Savior?" No, that's not possible. He's a mystical being way out there somewhere who forgave me of my sins and my name is written in a book, but that's a long way off. But then I learned that He is not a million miles away. He's beside me. What He wants is a relationship with me. So that was the next step in this journey.

Well, the process continued. In late 2012, the same question came up again, "Do you really trust Me?"

I still had many of the same addictions I had struggled with for years, including overwork, stress, and fatigue. I was absolutely driven to succeed in my job. During this time, I had been promoted to CEO over a portion of our company and was handling three senior executive assignments simultaneously. I averaged seventy-five to ninety hours of work per week. Many times I was away twenty-four/seven.

I told you I was a carrier of this addiction, and I'm sure some of you are, too, although you may not be aware of it. Let me ask you. Have you ever sent an e-mail to a co-worker, or someone that reports to you, on a Sunday or a Saturday or in the evening? What are you telling them? Speaking for myself, I was telling them, "I expect you to work twenty-four/seven. I expect you to work ninety hours a week." You know why? Because that's the behavior I was showing them. I wasn't telling them to honor the Sabbath. I wanted them to answer my e-mail on Sunday morning. I was expecting them to pour every ounce of their time and energy into work. I wanted my employees to be like me.

I had an extremely high-profile job, not only in Colorado but across the country. I had taken a relatively small portion of the company from about twenty million dollars in income to one hundred million dollars in about twelve months. It became a very fast-paced, highly successful business.

But then I heard from the Lord as loud as I've ever heard Him speak. He said, "This job will kill you." I knew that was true. My work was going to destroy my walk with the Lord. It was going to wreck my relationship with my family, and it was going to keep dragging me back in the direction of my addiction.

Instead, I followed the Lord's lead. I left the lucrative job and accepted another. From the beginning, I worked from my house in my jeans. I had dinner with my wife every night. I saw my daughter go off to school. I paid a price for the change financially, but my life took a *huge* leap forward. A *huge* leap forward.

So what have I done to replace the addictive behavior that seemed so important to me? I have a thirst to understand His significance. I have a peace I haven't known. I am still like a recovering alcoholic who can't drink. I still struggle occasionally with doubt and fear of failure, but I have a peace inside. I have found a reasonable balance in a job that I actually love. I have a better life every single day. I am debt-free. I am joyful, hopeful, and grateful.

My hypertension is gone. I take fewer medications at lower doses. My doctor was amazed and he said, "You have a lower blood pressure than you have had in ten years." My prediabetes is gone. Gone. Every lab result is normal for the first time since 2003. I also have friends who are holding me accountable.

But like any other addict, the temptations are still out there. You probably deal with them, too. I believe Christian men are no different from the rest of society in this regard. If anything, they may have a greater struggle to succeed than those with no faith. We are driven to be without fault in this world. But we have to admit that we are vulnerable and we need to lean on each other to stay on the right path.

I still have to be careful about money. I sold my place and

deposited the funds in the bank. Then I said to the Lord, "It's Yours." I want to invest in something that has significance. I knew the Lord wanted me to support a bus tour sponsored by the National Day of Prayer. I could have invested it in a 401(k). I could have invested it in retirement plans. But I have to ask myself, when I'm gone, will that money serve any purpose? I want to invest in my kids and in something that will revitalize my country. I hope I'll be blessed with many grandkids someday. I want them to have a country in which they can still pray freely, where marriage is still valued. I want to help promote Christian principles and values.

So I leave you with a verse that I've carried in my wallet for thirty years now. It's the same little piece of paper. I would take it out but it would probably fall into a million little pieces. I've read it every time I've changed positions and when I entered the military. It is so meaningful to me.

It says:

"Brothers and sisters, I do not consider myself yet to have taken hold of it. But one thing I do: Forgetting what is behind and straining toward what is ahead, I press on toward the goal to win the prize for which God has called me heavenward in Jesus Christ" (Phil. 3:13, 14).

My simple prayer for every man here and for every man in this country, is that they will listen to God and really, really trust Him.

Thank you and God bless you all.[4]

Comments by Craig Dance

I'm honored to be standing in the presence of so many godly men this morning. This is my sixth year to attend the National

Day of Prayer, and I feel a great sense of humility to be asked to speak today.

I'd like to tell you my story about God's faithfulness in my life. Let me give you a little background. I was born and raised in a Christian home in South Carolina. I know no more godly man than my father. He set a tremendous example in our home as a leader, but it took a long time for me to follow him.

To say I was the black sheep of the family would be an understatement. I had three brothers and I suppose I was "The Least Likely to Succeed." I went far astray as I was growing up. I wasn't a really wild party animal or anything like that, but I was flunking out of college and making some other big mistakes.

Then I met and fell in love with Hazel and we were married. She is a wonderful woman of God and she actually began mentoring me spiritually when we were dating and continued after we were married. I began to get on the right track. However, I had always been a bad money manager and Hazel began talking to me about the concept of tithing. We had very little money in those days. I'm not one of those guys who was born with a silver spoon in his mouth. Sometimes I didn't have a dollar to buy two hot dogs. So I told Hazel that we just couldn't afford to give, and we didn't.

Then one night in the late 1990s, my dad came by our house. At one point he said, "Son, until you grasp the concept of tithing, you're going to struggle with it for the rest of your life." And he challenged me very, very strongly on the doorstep of our home to read the book of Malachi, which speaks specifically about giving. He said, "Son, test God in this area of your life. The Scripture says that you can trust Him."

For some reason, I heard it that day and I made up my mind

that I would tithe thereafter even though we still had very little in the bank. So I started giving, and I want to tell you that God changed my life quickly. The Scripture says if He can't trust you with a small amount, then you can't be trusted with a lot. I didn't really understand that, but I began to pay tithe on what little I had. And very quickly my life began to turn around.

Here's how that happened. I grew up as a huge sports fan. I love sports and I wanted to be the next Brent Musburger, or the next Jim Nance. So as things started to get better in the late '90s, I went to work for a bus company called Good News Express. I was with them for two years and I learned the business. I still didn't have much money, but that's when the Lord put a dream in my heart to start my own company.

I put together a business plan to cater to sports teams, and it was based on three pillars. First, I wanted to make a better life for my family and to provide for my children. Second, as I learned the lessons of giving, I wanted to be able to sow resources back into God's kingdom and to give to the ministries I believed in. The third is that I wanted to make Champion Coach a very good place to work for drivers. I wanted to create an atmosphere of respect and kindness for them based on a decidedly Christian culture. Those were the three pillars of Champion Coach and that's where we started.

I still didn't have two nickels to rub together but this was my dream. Nevertheless, I was able to start Champion Coach in 1998, literally without a dime in my pocket. I borrowed one and a half million dollars at ten percent interest and financed the business for ten years. You do the math and tell me how we survived with no other capital. It was the grace of God.

We started operating with four buses in September. I took delivery of my eighth bus on December thirty-first, and we were on a roll. Champion Coach went from zero to eight buses in about ninety days. It took off from the first day.

I'm not going to tell you we didn't have struggles, because we certainly did. As a thirty-one-year-old with no business experience, it was difficult to manage eight and twelve and then finally fifteen buses, with thirty drivers. We operated out of the basement of my house. I certainly made some bad decisions, but I can honestly say that we never missed a payroll. There was never a day that I wondered if we would make it. I always knew that the Lord would provide for us as long as we obeyed Him and maintained the pillar of sowing back into the Kingdom.

We became a very respected company throughout the country, having contracts with Major League Baseball, the NFL, the NBA, and college football and basketball games. Champion became the exclusive carrier for the New York Yankees and served the Super Bowl and the Final Four basketball events. I just couldn't believe how God was blessing us.

Remember that I wanted to be a sportscaster but it never could have been. It wouldn't work for me to travel three hundred days a year or to call a hundred and eighty baseball games a year, because I'm a family man. My priority was to be home with my family and be a good husband and a good father to my children. So I never could have done that. Instead, God called me to fulfill His perfect will for my life.

But there was a big challenge to come. On August 3, 2011, I received a call from one of our largest customers. He said, "I just heard from CBS Sports and they're looking for a quality bus company. I told them to call you."

I said, "That's great. I'll talk to them."

Later that day, the executive director of CBS Sports called

me. That was the beginning of several weeks of negotiations that involved our company. It was unbelievable. They brought me to CBS headquarters in New York where the details were laid out. They had the rights to the SEC championship game, the LSU Alabama game, the Masters Tournament, the Super Bowl, the Final Four basketball tournament, Major League Baseball, and many other national sporting events. It was everything I could have dreamed about. Champion Coach was to be "wrapped" and seen by millions of people on network television. The deal would continue for two years.

Finally, on the Friday before Labor Day, we reached an agreement with CBS Sports to make Champion Coach the CBS SEC Cruiser.

But it didn't stop there. The president of CBS Television stopped me in the lobby of a hotel and said, "I want to promote CBS Television on a sixty-day bus tour and showcase our new fall lineup this summer. We want to visit all of our affiliates all around the country. We're going to open the tour on national television with the Boston Pops Festival on July Fourth." George said he wanted to talk to me about providing the bus to do this.

I said, "Wow, that sounds interesting." But I began to feel uneasy. I was thinking, "Is this something I should be involved in?"

There is a distinct difference between CBS Sports and CBS Television programming, which produces trash and things my family won't watch. Could I allow my bus to be wrapped with depictions of violence, scantily clad women, and other filth? This is not what Champion Coach has stood for.

I didn't tell the executive about my reluctance. I just said, "Fine. That sounds great. We'll talk about it." It was clear that the sports deal and the television tour were connected, and George held the key to our 2012 deal with CBS Sports. It was a lucrative deal for us.

Negotiations moved on and George stayed in touch with me. In January 2012, he called and said, "We've got to get 'The Buzz Tour' off the ground." He wanted to know what Champion Coach was going to do.

"Well, George," I said, "I'll be out in LA in February."

That's where CBS is based.

I said, "Why don't I come out and we can talk about this?"

He said, "That'd be great! I'll put you on the schedule."

Hazel and I flew to Los Angeles and had lunch together. We prayed about the decision we faced, and then we went to CBS.

We met again with George. We discussed the deal but didn't finalize it.

After leaving the meeting, Hazel and I again asked each other if this was something we could feel good about doing.

We returned to South Carolina and George began calling again and sending e-mails. Before I knew it, other executives from CBS were flying down from New York to our offices. They were bringing stars from television shows to our little office in Greenville, South Carolina. We continued to pray about all this and we just could not get peace that God gives us when we're doing the right thing. It just was not there. But what would I do with CBS pursuing us? I thought maybe I'd send them the contract and raise the price so high they would never accept it. I wanted to take the easy way out.

I began seeking counsel from Christian leaders, including people who were wiser than I was: my father, my pastor and the chairman of Joni and Friends, and others. And we all began to pray and seek God's will. We finally felt the Lord telling me to call CBS and let them know where we stood on the issues.

So I picked up the phone and I called the CBS president. I said, "George, it's Craig. Listen, I need to have a heart-to-heart with you. I need to tell you where I stand. I'm a Christian. I'm born-again. And my company promotes good, honest, clean values in America."

I said, "I just can't align myself or my company with some of the things that you guys are producing there at CBS." I said, "I'm mainly concerned about the wrap of the bus. What will it look like? What are you going to put on it? Is it going to include violence? Is it going to show scantily clad women? What it is going to be?"

He said, "Craig, we're like-minded. You and I are like-minded."

I'm sitting there thinking, "We are?!"

He said, "I would like to think that CBS does not have any shows like that. And no problem, we'll work with you. You can have the final say on the wrap."

Let me tell you why this businessman said we were like-minded and how he could say it so easily. It is because the popular culture accepts profanity, violence, sex, and homosexuality on TV. It isn't shocking anymore.

So we finished our call and I went in and told my wife about it. We called our pastor and my dad again and we talked and prayed about the dilemma.

About that time the first wrap design on the bus came out, and it had a guy holding a gun. So I sent an e-mail to the designers and I said, "I talked to George about this. We cleared this. I won't accept it." So they sent another wrap. They took the bad stuff off.

But then I walked into Hazel's office and I looked down at the entertainment section of *USA Today*. The headline read, "CBS unveils fall lineup for 2012." We read the story. It said CBS will have a new show in the fall called *Partners*. And you can imagine what *Partners* was about... two gay men.

I knew at that point that we had reached the end of the road with CBS. So I sent an e-mail to the designer and I said, "Will *Partners* be promoted on our bus or in any way?" and the lady asked, "Is there a problem?" And I said, "Yes."

This was around five o'clock in the afternoon. George was in LA. So I went home. I told Hazel what had happened and I said, "You know, we're going to walk away from the deal. We're going to walk. We're going to stand up for righteousness and do what's right here."

So the next morning, I got to the office about eight o'clock and George from CBS television was on the phone. I answered, "George, how are you this morning?"

He said, "Fine, Craig, and you?"

"Great."

"Listen, Craig," he said. These were his exact words: "Craig we have to compromise on this. We have to compromise."

I sat down and took a deep breath and I thought, "Lord, help me." I said, "George, there will be no compromise on this issue." I said, "I told you where I stand, and I tell you, I think I need to move on." I didn't mention the topic of gays and homosexuality when I talked to him. I mean, it's a touchy subject for people, particularly in the entertainment industry. And at the time CBS didn't have any shows promoting gays that I could find, so I didn't mention it. Now I was kind of in a bind, because I had waffled about it. But I said, "There will be no compromise. The Bible is clear. Marriage is between one man and one woman and we can't compromise."

I said, "I'll be happy to let you out of the contract and I'll walk away from it, but Champion Coach cannot do it."

He said, "Craig, we'll work it out. We'll work it out. Call you back in an hour."

I went in and told Hazel, "I think they're going to work it out. They respect me."

She said, "Honey, they respect you but you'll receive another call shortly from George."

And I did. He called me and said, "Craig, I respect your opinion but CBS cannot promote our shows for the views of one man. So we ask you to let us out of the contract."

I agreed to it and said, "I'm sorry, George, but what Champion Coach stands for and what we've been promoting for fifteen years is far more important to us than the lucrative deal we've struck."

I don't know how many hundreds of thousands of dollars we would've received from CBS Sports, but it didn't matter because I knew that the Scripture was clear on all the issues. There was no black and white. I mean... it was just clear and I was convicted. I knew it was time to take a stand for righteousness.

George told me as he hung up the phone, "Listen, Craig, I like you a lot. You can go ahead and do your deal with CBS Sports. You'll be able to do that." But I knew it was over. And so I hung up the phone and went in and I talked to Hazel. I told her what had happened and we were fine with it. There was the peace that God promises in His Word. It surpasses all understanding.

But there was one more thing I had to do. I had to make a phone call to all the guys at CBS Sports. They had been my friends. They had trusted me to take their vision for the CBS Cruiser into the 2012 season. They had placed a lot of faith in me and they knew I would get it done. And so I had to call them.

I didn't look forward to that call because I thought they'd tell me I was an idiot and how could you do this to us? But the guy who had been planning the sports events, who is an atheist, was completely silent for a minute. Then he said, "Wow. I've never heard anybody put their money where their mouth is like that in all my life." That is exactly what he said.

He continued, "I respect you and I hate it, but I will do everything I can to push the sports deal through in spite of this. I don't know where the bureaucracy will fall but I will try to make it happen." Each person I called treated me with respect.

I just want to say to all of you who are here today, that I want to encourage you in your business. If you're in a moral dilemma like this and you take a stand for righteousness, you will not regret it. In the end, righteousness will prevail.

The year 2012 turned out to be the best year we've had in the history of Champion Coach. We didn't miss the CBS money. Because of that blessing we've been able to take that second pillar to the next level. We provided buses for the Family Research Council, Joni and Friends, *Family Talk*, the National Day of Prayer, *Focus on the Family*, and others. We tested God, and He was faithful.

So this is what we're doing now. Our new project is to promote prayer for America. This is all about righteousness and standing in the gap. I just want to leave you with one verse of Scripture that I read this morning: It says, "From everlasting to everlasting the Lord's love is with those who fear him and his righteousness with his children's children" (Ps. 103:17).

Securing righteousness for my children and their children is what it's all about.

God bless you all.[5]

—∿∿—

Weren't those inspiring remarks from Russ and Craig? I want to thank them for sharing their personal stories with us, and for their willingness to reveal not only their triumphs along the way, but also the dark side of their journeys. I have included their accounts in this book because their experiences are highly relevant to other men. I have talked to thousands of guys of all ages, and I can tell you that those who are middle-aged or older usually harbor deep regrets about their priorities. Most of them understand that now. Younger men haven't yet realized the mistakes they are making, but eventually they will. The details are different in each case, but the roads they have traveled look very familiar.

Those who have "Type A" personalities have bumped their heads on the same old rock. They began adult life with an unquenchable thirst for power, possessions, success, achievement, and position, which led to constant time pressure, exhaustion, marital conflict and/or divorce, and ultimately, alienation from children. If something doesn't happen to turn them around, the end result will often be chronic illness, despair, and death. Russ saw that coming.

Let me speak directly now to young men, particularly, about another trap that lies in your paths. Read carefully, please. Whatever you ache for, whether it is money, status, glory, sex, influence, or all the above, I promise you that Satan will appear to offer it to you. He knows your vulnerabilities, and he will put what you lust for right in front of you. Then he will entice you to take it, as he did with Eve in the Garden of Eden. But as it was with her and later with Adam, you won't get the prize without paying a dear price for it. You may even have to sell your soul to bring it home. You may begin to compromise your belief system, such as with dishonesty, sexual flirtation, excessive drinking, and exploitation of others. You might be among countless men who ignore the sexual and emotional needs of your wife. That can lead to your own inner loneliness, which gives rise to pornography, gambling, and other cheap thrills. It's all part of the package.

Imagine the temptation Craig was under. He had within his grasp every possible business success he could have dreamed about. It came from one of the most powerful institutions ever built, CBS Television and CBS Sports. All he had to do was allow his company to be used to promote evil in various forms. The allure couldn't have been more seductive. Thank God he had a great wife and father who stood by him during his trial by fire. He wavered for a moment, but then made the right decision in the nick of time. Now the Lord is blessing him abundantly—not just financially, but in his marriage, his personal life, and the spirituality of his children. How could CBS have competed with such rich benefits?

The good news is that men don't have to self-destruct. Russ and Craig recognized where they were headed. Their wives were somewhere praying for them. Men are fools who won't listen to the concerned voices of the women God gave them. That is one of the most important messages found in these two stories.

If I have sounded somewhat preachy in this commentary, please remember that I almost made the same mistakes when I was a young man. Opportunity beckoned me from every side, and I became almost drunk with its promises. Yes Sir, I was headed down the same rocky road. My wife Shirley helped to open my eyes and my father pulled me back from the edge. He got to the heart of the problem when he wrote, "Failure to win your children to Christ would make mere success in your profession a very pale and washed-out affair, indeed. But this prayer demands time—time that cannot be given if it is all signed and conscripted and laid on the altar of career ambition."

I awakened in time to reverse course. Will you? That is my prayer for you.

CHAPTER TWELVE

Spiritual Training of Children

Our theme has been to examine the most important task in parenting, which is to win children to Jesus Christ. That teaching process is more difficult today than in the past, given the cultural depravity of our day and the efforts by unscrupulous men and women who seek to manipulate them. Distortions of the truth are everywhere, in children's secular literature, Saturday morning cartoons, movies, music, some public school classrooms, and throughout culture. Therefore, I am repeating some commonly asked questions about spiritual concerns and my suggestions in reply.

Q: What is the most important period in the spiritual training of young children?

A: Each era is significant, but I believe the fifth year is often the most critical. Until that time, children believe in God because their parents say it is the right thing to do. They accept the reality of Jesus, in much the same way they believe in the fable of Santa Claus. Children don't think critically about how it is possible for the man in a red suit to circle the entire globe in a single night, or how a sleigh can be pulled across the sky by eight flying reindeer, one with a glowing red nose. It is ridiculous, of course, but a three- or four-year-old youngster will accept it uncritically and innocently if Mom and Dad say it is true.

At about five or six years of age, however, boys and girls begin to think more critically about what they are told. Some of them come to a fork in the road at about that time. Either they begin to internalize what they've been taught and make it their own, or else the Bible stories become like the fables that don't exist in the real world. It is a time for careful instruction at home and in church.

I certainly don't mean to imply that parents should wait until children are in school to begin their spiritual training. Nor are subsequent years insignificant. But I am convinced that our most thoughtful efforts to teach kids about Jesus should occur at that time, and our best Sunday school teachers ought to be assigned to those between five or six years old. There will be crucial crossroads after that, to be sure, but this one is first.

Q: I believe it is best for me to let my child decide for himself on matters related to God. Wouldn't we be forcing our religion down his throat if we tell him what he must believe?

A: Let me answer the question with an illustration from nature. A little gosling (baby goose) has a peculiar characteristic that is relevant at this point. Shortly after he hatches from his shell he will become attached, or imprinted, to the first thing that he sees moving near him. From that time forward, the gosling follows that particular object when it moves in his vicinity. Ordinarily, it becomes imprinted to the mother goose that was on hand to witness the new generation.

If she is removed, however, the gosling will settle for any mobile substitute, whether alive or not. In fact, a gosling will become most easily attached to a blue football bladder dragged by it on a string. A week later, it will fall in line behind the bladder as it scoots by.

Time is the critical factor in this process. The gosling is vulnerable to imprinting for only a few seconds after it hatches from the shell; if that opportunity is lost, it cannot be regained later. In other words, there is a brief but critical period in the life of a gosling when this instinctual learning is possible.

Coming back to your question now, there is also a critical period when certain kinds of instruction are made easier in the lives of children. Although humans have no instincts (only drives, reflexes, urges, etc.), there is a brief period during childhood when youngsters are vulnerable to religious training. Their concepts of right and wrong are formulated during this time, and their view of God begins to solidify. As in the case of the gosling, the opportunity of that period must be seized when the child is ready developmentally. Leaders of the Catholic Church have been widely quoted as saying, "Give us a child until he is seven years old, and we'll have him for life"; they are usually correct, because permanent attitudes can be instilled during these seven vulnerable years.

Unfortunately, however, the opposite is also true. The absence or misapplication of instruction through the prime time period may place a severe limitation on the depth of a child's later devotion to God. When parents withhold indoctrination from their small children, allowing them to decide for themselves, the adults are almost guaranteeing that their youngsters will decide in the negative. If parents want their children to have a meaningful faith, they must give up any misguided attempts at objectivity. Children listen closely to discover just how much their parents believe what they preach. Any indecision or ethical confusion from the parent is likely to be magnified in the child.

After the middle-adolescent age (ending at about fifteen years), children sometimes resent heavy-handedness about anything—including what to believe. But if the early exposure has been properly conducted, they should have an anchor to steady them. Their early indoctrination, then, is the key to the spiritual attitudes they carry into adulthood.

I suggest you give up any misguided notions of letting children decide for themselves. You may regret doing that later on.

Q: You have said that children of godly parents sometimes go into severe rebellion and never return to the faith they were taught. I have seen that happen to some wonderful families who loved the Lord and were committed to the church. Still, it appears contradictory to Scripture. How do you interpret Proverbs 22:6 (KJV), which says, "Train up a child in the way he should go: and when he is old, he will not depart from it"? Doesn't that verse mean, as it implies, that the children of wise and dedicated Christian parents will never be lost? Doesn't it promise that all wayward offspring will return, sooner or later, to the fold?

A: I wish Solomon's message to us could be interpreted that definitively. I know that the common understanding of the passage is to accept it as a divine guarantee, but it was not expressed in that context. Psychiatrist John White, writing in his excellent book, *Parents in Pain*, makes the case that the proverbs were never intended to be absolute promises from God. Instead, they are "probabilities" of things that are likely to occur. Solomon, who wrote the wonderful book of Proverbs, was the wisest man on the earth at that time. His purpose was to convey his divinely inspired observations on the way human nature and God's universe work. A given set of circumstances can be expected to produce a set of specific consequences. Unfortunately, several of these observations, including Proverbs 22:6, have been lifted out of that context and made to stand alone as promises from God. If we insist on that interpretation, then we must explain why so many other proverbs do not inevitably prove accurate. For example:

"Lazy hands make a man poor, but diligent hands bring wealth" (10:4). (Have you ever met a diligent—but poor—Christian? I have.)

"The blessing of the Lord brings wealth, and he adds no trouble to it" (10:22).

"The fear of the Lord adds length to life, but the years of the wicked are cut short" (10:27). (I have watched some beautiful children die with a Christian testimony on their lips.)

"No harm befalls the righteous, but the wicked have their fill of trouble" (12:21).

"Plans fail for lack of counsel, but with many advisers they succeed" (15:22).

"Gray hair is a crown of splendor; it is attained by a righteous life" (16:31).

"The lot is cast into the lap, but its every decision is from the Lord" (16:33).

"A tyrannical ruler lacks judgment, but he who hates ill-gotten gain will enjoy a long life" (28:16).

We can all think of exceptions to the statements above. To repeat, the proverbs appear to represent likelihoods rather than absolutes with God's personal guarantee attached.

This interpretation of Scripture is somewhat controversial among laymen, but less so among biblical scholars. For example, *Bible Knowledge Commentary: Old Testament*, prepared by the faculty of the Dallas Theological Seminary, accepts the understanding I have suggested. This commentary is recognized for its intense commitment to the literal interpretation of God's Word, yet this is what the theologians wrote.

Some parents, however, have sought to follow this directive but without this result. Their children have strayed from the godly training the parents gave them. This illustrates the nature of a proverb. A proverb is a literary device whereby a general truth is brought to bear on a specific situation. Many of the proverbs are not absolute guarantees, for they express truths that are necessarily conditioned by prevailing circumstances. For example, verses 3, 4, 9, 11, 16, and 29 of Proverbs 22 do not express promises that are always binding. Though the proverbs are generally and usually true, occasional exceptions may be noted. This may be because of the self-will or deliberate disobedience of an individual who chooses to go his own way—the way of folly instead of the way of wisdom. For that he is held responsible. It is generally true, however, that most children who are brought up in

Christian homes, under the influence of godly parents who teach and live God's standards, follow that training.

Those who believe that Proverbs 22:6 offers a guarantee of salvation for the next generation have assumed, in essence, that a child can be programmed so thoroughly as to determine his course inevitably. If they bring him up "in the way he should go," the outcome is certain. But think about that for a moment. Didn't the Creator handle Adam and Eve with infinite wisdom and love? He made no mistakes in "fathering" them. They were also harbored in a perfect environment with none of the pressures we face. They had no in-law problems, no monetary needs, no frustrating employers, no television, no pornography, no alcohol or drugs, no peer pressure, and no sorrow. They had no excuses! Nevertheless, they ignored the explicit warning from God and stumbled into sin. If it were ever possible to avoid the ensnarement of evil, it would have occurred in that sinless world. But it didn't. God in His love gave Adam and Eve a choice between good and evil, and they abused it. Will He now withhold that same freedom from your children? No. Ultimately, they will make their own choices. That time of decision is a breathtaking moment for parents, when everything they have taught appears to be on the line. But it must come for us all.

Q: You obviously feel very strongly about this misinterpretation of Scripture. What are its implications?

A: I am most concerned for dedicated and sincere Christian parents whose grown sons and daughters have rebelled against God and their own families. Many of these mothers and fathers did the best they could to raise their children properly, but they lost them anyway. That situation produces enormous guilt in itself, quite apart from scriptural understandings. They are led to believe that God has promised—absolutely guaranteed—the spiritual welfare of children whose parents do their jobs properly. What are they to conclude, then, in light of continued rebellion and sin in the next generation? The message is inescapable: It must be their fault! They have damned their own kids by failing to keep their half of the bargain. They have sent their beloved children to hell by their parenting failures. This thought is so terrible for a sensitive believer that it could actually undermine his or her sanity.

I simply do not believe God intended for the total responsibility for sin in the next generation to fall on the backs of vulnerable parents. When we look at the entire Bible, we find no support for that extreme position. Cain's murder of Abel was not blamed on his parents. Joseph was a godly man and his brothers were rascals, yet their father and mothers (Jacob, Leah, and Rachel) were not held accountable for the differences between them. The saintly Samuel raised rebellious children, yet he was not charged with their sin. And in the New Testament, the father of the Prodigal Son was never accused of raising his son improperly. The boy was apparently old enough to make his own headstrong decision, and his father did not stand in his way. This good man never repented of any wrongdoing—nor did he need to.

It is not my intention to let parents off the hook when they have been slovenly or uncommitted during their child-rearing years. There is at least one biblical example of God's wrath falling on a father who failed to discipline and train his sons. I have already mentioned the account of Eli, who raised undisciplined and rebellions sons. Much of the blame rested on the Old Priest.

Obviously, the Lord takes our parenting tasks seriously and expects us to do likewise. But He does not intend for us to grovel in guilt for circumstances beyond our control!

Q: Our three children were prayed for before they were conceived, and we have held their names before the Lord almost every day of their lives. Yet our middle daughter has chosen to reject our faith and do things she knows are wrong. She's living with a twice-divorced man and apparently has no intention of marrying him. She has had at least two abortions that we know about, and her language is disgraceful. My wife and I have prayed until we're exhausted, and yet she has shown no interest in returning to the church. At times, I become very angry at God for allowing this terrible thing to happen. I have wept until there are just no more tears. Tell me what intercessory prayer accomplishes, if anything. Is there a realm into which the Father will not intrude?

A: I can certainly understand your pain. Perhaps more people have become disillusioned with God over the waywardness of a son or daughter than any other issue. There is nothing more important to most Christian parents than the salvation of their children. Every other goal and achievement in life is anemic and insignificant compared to this transmission of faith to their offspring. That is the only way the two generations can be together throughout eternity, and those parents, like you, have been praying day and night for spiritual awakening. Unfortunately, if God does not answer those prayers quickly, there is a tendency to blame Him and to struggle with intense feelings of bitterness. The "betrayal barrier" claims another victim!

Often, this anger at the Lord results from a misunderstanding of what He will and won't do in the lives of those for whom we intercede. The key question is this: will God require our offspring to serve Him if they choose a path of rebellion? It is a critically important question.

Let me explain again that God will not force Himself on anyone. If that were His inclination, no person would ever be lost. Second Peter 3:9 says, "He is patient with you, not wanting anyone to perish, but everyone to come to repentance." Nevertheless, to claim this great salvation, there is a condition. An individual must reach out and take it. He or she must repent of sins and believe on the name of the Lord Jesus Christ. Without that step of faith, the gift of forgiveness and eternal life is impossible.

Now let me deal with your question about what intercessory prayer accomplishes. Referring again to Dr. White's insightful book *Parents in Pain*, now unfortunately out of print, he wrote:

> Here lies a key to understanding how we may pray for our own children or for anyone else. We may ask with every confidence that God will open the eyes of the morally and spiritually blind. We may ask that the self-deceptions which sinners hide behind may be burned away in the fierce light of truth, that dark caverns may be rent asunder to let the sunlight pour in, that self-disguises may be stripped from a man or woman to reveal the horror of their nakedness in the holy light of God. We may ask above all that the glory of the face of Christ will shine through the spiritual blindness caused by the god of this world (Corinthians 4:4). All of this we can ask with every assurance that God will not only hear but will delight to answer.
>
> But we may not ask him to force a man, woman, or child to love and trust him. To deliver them from overwhelming temptation: yes. To give them every opportunity: yes.

To reveal his beauty, his tenderness, his forgiveness: yes. But to force a man against his will to bow the knee: not in this life. And to force a man to trust him: never.

Said another way, the Lord will not save a person against his will, but He has a thousand ways of making him more willing. Our prayers unleash the power of God in the life of another individual. We have been granted the privilege of entering into intercessory prayer for our loved ones and of holding their names and faces before the Father. In return, He makes the all-important choices crystal clear to that individual and brings positive influences into his or her life to maximize the probability of doing what is right. Beyond that, I believe He will not go.

Q: My wife and I have been praying for the salvation of our children for more than twenty-five years, and there is no sign that God has even heard those prayers. I know He loves our family, but I'm quite discouraged. Can you tell us anything that will jump-start our faith again?

A: I have an encouraging word for you and others who have asked the Lord for a miracle that hasn't yet come. It is found in one of my favorite Scriptures located in the book of Genesis. You'll remember that when Abraham was seventy-five years of age he began receiving promises from God that he would become the father of a great nation and that in him, all the nations of the world would be blessed. That was great news to an aging man and his barren wife, Sarah, who longed to be a mother.

Yet these exciting promises were followed by Sarah's continued infertility and many years of silence from God. What she and Abraham faced at this point was a classic case of "God contradicting God." The Lord hadn't honored His word or explained

His delay. The facts didn't add up. The pieces didn't fit. Sarah had gone through menopause, effectively ending her hope of motherhood. By then, she and her husband were old, and we can assume that their sexual passion had diminished. There was no realistic probability that they were to be given an heir.

Abraham's response at that discouraging moment was described nearly two thousand years later in the writings of the apostle Paul. These are the inspirational words that he wrote:

> Without weakening in his faith, [Abraham] faced the fact that his body was as good as dead—since he was about a hundred years old—and that Sarah's womb was also dead. Yet he did not waver through unbelief regarding the promise of God, but was strengthened in his faith and gave glory to God, being fully persuaded that God had power to do what he had promised. This is why "it was credited to him as righteousness." (Romans 4:19–22)

In other words, Abraham believed God even when He made no sense. The facts clearly said, "It is impossible for this thing to happen." The Lord had made "empty promises" for nearly twenty-five years, and still there was no sign of their fulfillment. Unanswered questions and troubling contradictions swirled through the air. Nevertheless, Abraham "did not waver through unbelief." Why? Because he was convinced that God could transcend reason and factual evidence. And this is why he is called the "father of our faith."

Isn't that a wonderful example of faith under fire? It should give us courage to retain our spiritual confidence even when the pieces don't fit. Remember that with God, even when nothing is happening, something is happening. And if we don't waver, someday we'll understand, and "it will be credited to [us] as righteousness" for our faithfulness.

Stay on your knees. And hang on to your faith like a life preserver! The Lord is at work in the lives of your children, even though you see no evidence of it at the moment.

Q: My wife and I are new Christians, and we now realize that we raised our kids by the wrong principles. They're grown now, but we continue to worry about the past, and we feel great regret for our failures as parents. Is there anything we can do at this late date?

A: Let me deal first with the awful guilt you are obviously carrying. There's hardly a parent alive who does not have some regrets and painful memories of their failures as a mother or a father. Children are infinitely complex, and we can no more be perfect parents than we can be perfect human beings. The pressures of living are often enormous. We get tired and irritated; we are influenced by our physical bodies and our emotions, which sometimes prevent us from saying the right things and being the models we should be. We don't always handle our children as unemotionally as we wish we had, and it's very common to look back a year or two later and see how wrong we were in the way we approached a problem.

All of us experience these failures! No one does the job perfectly! That's why each of us should get alone with God and say:

"Lord, You know my inadequacies. You know my weaknesses, not only in parenting, but in every area of my life. I did the best I could, but it wasn't good enough. As You broke the fishes and the loaves to feed the five thousand, now take my meager effort and use it to bless my family. Make up for the things I did wrong. Satisfy the needs that I have not satisfied. Wrap Your great arms around my children, and draw them close to You. And be there when they stand at the great crossroads between right and wrong. All I can give is my best, and I've done that. Therefore, I submit to You my children and myself and the job I did as a parent. The outcome now belongs to You."

I know the Father will honor that prayer, even for parents whose job is finished. The Lord does not want you to suffer from guilt over events you can no longer influence. The past is the past. Let it die, never to be resurrected. Give the situation to God, and let Him have it. I think you'll be surprised to learn that you're no longer alone!

Forgetting what is behind and straining toward what is ahead, I press on toward the goal to win the prize for which God has called me heavenward in Christ Jesus. (Philippians 3:13–14)

Q: I am a grandmother who is blessed to have fourteen grand-children. I often take care of them and love just having them over. However, I would like to do more for them than just babysit. What can I do to really make an impact on their lives?

A: Above all else, I would hope you would help lead your grand-children to Jesus Christ. You are in a wonderful position to do that. My grandmother had a profound impact on my spiritual development—even greater in my early years than my father, who was a minister. She talked about the Lord every day and made Him seem like a very dear friend who lived in our house. I will never forget the conversations we had about heaven and how wonderful it would be to live there throughout eternity.

That little lady is on the other side today, waiting for the rest of her family to join her in that beautiful city.

You can have that kind of impact on your family, too. Grandparents have been given powerful influence on their grandchildren if they will take the time to invest in their lives. There is so much to be accomplished while they are young. Another of the great contributions you can make is to preserve the heritage of your family by describing its history to children and acquainting them with their ancestors.

The lyrics of an African folk song say that when an old person dies, it's as if a library has burned down. It is true. There's a richness of history in your memory of earlier days that will be lost if it isn't passed on to the next generation.

To preserve this heritage, you should tell them true stories of days gone by. Share about your faith, about your early family experiences, about the obstacles you overcame or the failures you suffered. Those recollections bring a family together and give it a sense of identity.

The stories of your past, of your childhood, of your courtship with their grandfather, etc., can be treasures to your grandchildren. Unless you share those experiences with them, that part of their history will be gone forever. Take the time to make yesterday come alive for the kids in your family, and by all means, pass your faith along to the next generation.

Finally, these last two questions are about violence and its effect on children.

Q: Dr. Dobson, I am extremely concerned about my children, ages six and seven, in the aftermath of the horrible killing in Newtown, Connecticut. They don't know the details, but they've heard at school that "something awful" happened to many boys and girls. They are asking about it and I don't know what to tell them. How should I handle this tragic situation?

A: The massacre of children that shocked the nation is almost beyond comprehension. Parents everywhere are grieving and trying to decide how to respond to their children's' unanswerable questions. Maybe these suggestions will be helpful.

I think it is important to tell your young children that there are some very bad people in the world who do hurtful things to others. Sometimes boys and girls are the ones who get hurt. That is what happened in Newtown, Connecticut. I wouldn't tell them that children were killed, or murdered, or that something else unthinkable happened at a school. Don't overstate it in a way that will terrify them. But they do need answers.

At this point, you have to walk a very narrow path. On the one hand, you want to teach them to stay away from strangers and to tell you if anything scares them. On the other hand, you can't afford to make them feel like the world is out to get them and that they are in constant danger. You want them to be cautious without being fearful of all adults.

Everything depends on your demeanor. If you are anxious and fearful, they will be, too. Children take their cues from their parents. Try to discuss the subject without showing that you are extremely upset. Don't cry or make your kids think you are not able to protect them. Their security is in your hands. They also need to know that the crisis is over.

Tell them, "Police came to get the bad man and he will never hurt anyone again." Assure your children of your love and remind them that God gave them mommies and daddies to protect them, and that you watch out for them every hour of every day. It is why you sometimes have to say no to their requests.

If you have a strong faith, I think you should then turn to Jesus. Tell them He cares for each of us and that He will hear us when we ask for protection. He knows our names and is with us at all times. The Bible also tells us He especially loves little children.

My six-year-old grandson, Lincoln, has been having some bad dreams about monsters. He has been waking up crying at night. When he told his dad about it two weeks ago, Ryan began reading Psalm 91 with him every night before going to sleep. This is a very comforting passage, and Lincoln has had very few nightmares since they began reading it.

I have paraphrased Psalm 91 below, taken from *The Message*. You might want to use it, or another version. *The Message* is written for adults, obviously, and might need to be edited for children as I have done:

Those who sit down in the God's presence will spend the night in His shadow. He's my protection. I trust in Him and I'm safe! He rescues me from hidden traps, and shields me from every danger. His huge arms encircle me—under them I'm perfectly safe; his arms protect me from harm. I fear nothing—not even wild animals at night.

Bad people who try to scare me will get pushed away. Even evil can't get close to me. It can't get through the door. God ordered his angels to guard me wherever I go. If I stumble, they'll catch me; their job is to keep me from falling. I'll walk unharmed among lions and snakes, and kick them out of my way. "If I hold on to God," He says, "I'll get you out of any trouble. I'll give you the best of care if you'll only get to know and trust me."

Call me and I'll answer. I'll be at your side in bad times. I'll rescue you and give you a long life, and give you a long drink of salvation!

I've taken some liberties with the Scripture here, but I think I've been faithful to the context. After you have read this psalm, I suggest you pray together and thank Jesus for loving and caring for us. Give thanks also for the angels that stand guard over us as we sleep. And give thanks for mommies and daddies who also love and take care of their children. Ask Jesus to help us learn to trust him more. Finally, on alternate nights, read or quote the Lord's Prayer with your children.

Every circumstance is different, and the suggested wording offered here varies with the age, maturity, and security of each child. What I've written was designed for kids in elementary school, and is just a guide to be modified to meet the needs of a particular boy or girl.

I hope this is helpful. What a shame that we have to deal with tragedies like this, but I'm afraid it is the world we live in.

Q: What do you think caused the killer in Newtown to do such unthinkable things?

A: I am not familiar with the particulars of this massacre, but I can speak to the question generally. America has become a dangerous place partially because of the violence we tolerate. Even young children grow up today playing violent video games and watching unwholesome cable television, Hollywood movies, MTV, and many other depictions of dramatized murder, rape, drug usage, etc. Children are exposed to these influences from early ages. Millions of them come home to empty houses every afternoon and watch unsavory stuff that should never be witnessed by kids.

The producers and advertisers of violent "entertainment" have insisted for decades that children are not harmed by dramatized violence. Of course they are wrong. Why would advertisers spend billions of dollars to get their products before the public, including children? It is because what we see and hear influences how we behave and who we are. One quick glance of Reese's Pieces in the movie *E.T.* sent America's kids rushing out to buy the candy. How ridiculous to think that a steady diet of killing and torturing and knifing innocent victims would not warp the morals and character of the nation's children. They have a way of growing up, as we know, and ordinary citizens pay a huge price for what we have done to our innocent little ones.

There is another dimension that should be noted. Violence in adulthood is often related to other ways children have been warped and wounded. Boys and girls who were sexually and verbally abused or horribly neglected when they were young often grow up angry and vicious. That results from the production of prodigious amounts of the stress hormone cortisol. It floods the brain during times of severe pain or fear and causes irreversible damage to portions of the brain. One of the consequences of this damage is an inability of teens and young adults to "feel" for others. Many of them can kill without any emotional response to what they are doing. They have no conscience.

Millions of dollars in behavioral research has been invested to understand this phenomenon. One of the consequences of childhood terror and emotional pain is the creation of violent psychopaths. Many of these individuals were not cared for when they were babies, and now they wreak havoc on innocent victims. We can do better with the children entrusted to our care.

CHAPTER THIRTEEN

The Deeper Meaning of Legacy

We come now to the essence of my message, which takes us back to the meaning of *legacy*. This word has several definitions, but the most basic among them refers to "an inheritance." It's what we hope to bequeath to our benefactors. Every adult should be thinking about what he or she will pass along, because we all know you can't take it with you. Someone asked the friends of a very rich man who had died, "How much money did Ralph leave behind?" The answer, of course, is "All of it." Job said, "Naked I came from my mother's womb, and naked I will depart." That thought is kind of depressing, isn't it? Nevertheless, it confronts us all.

A popular bumper sticker reads, "He who dies with the most toys, wins." It's a lie. It should read, "He who dies with the most toys, dies anyway." I hope you agree that a lifetime invested in the accumulation of worldly possessions will have been wasted if that turns out to be your primary reason for living. When all has been said and done, it won't matter.

So let me ask you directly: Have you decided what assets you will leave to those you love? Is it money, or fame, or property, or gold, or diamonds, or a yacht, or priceless works of art, or stocks and bonds, or investments, or other aspects of wealth? Have you worked feverishly for decades to provide for those who haven't earned what you'll give them? Do you want to remove all the challenges and lessons that would otherwise help them to succeed? What will be the net effect of your financial gifts in years to come?

It is a moot question for most people, because they will never be able to pass along large estates to their children and grandchildren. Just getting by has been a struggle, especially in this economy. However, if parents do have significant assets to leave behind, research indicates that giving abundantly to offspring is risky business, although very few people seem to believe it.

I have in my library a book titled *Rich Kids*,[1] by sociologist John Sedgwick. He reports a sociological study of young men and women who inherit large estates. The findings are striking and they are not good. The case studies presented indicate that those who come into wealth often fall prey to many temptations. They are more likely to become alcoholics, philanderers, gamblers, or at best, self-possessed and selfish people. The very characteristics that made their parents and grandparents successful, notably hard work, frugality, wise investments, and careful planning, are often diminished in the next generation. This isn't always true, of course, but it certainly can be.

Human history also confirms the dangerous influence of money. Men and women have lusted for it, killed for it, died for it, and gone to hell for it. Money has come between the best of friends and brought down the proud and mighty. Even more important is what riches can do to the relationships between husbands and wives. If money is inherited by a woman, for example, her husband can lose his motivation to provide and care for her. She doesn't need him as she did when they married. You may not agree with this, but I can tell you as a psychologist that it is true. A man's masculinity can be assaulted by becoming unnecessary at home.

Shirley and I have been married for fifty-four years, and one of my greatest satisfactions in living has been the privilege of caring for, supporting, and "being there" for this lady since we were young. I enjoy her dependence on me and I'm also dependent on her in different but important ways. One reason our bond has been so strong is because we need each other emotionally, physically, and spiritually. Remember the popular song whose lyrics proclaim, "People who need people are the luckiest people in the world."² I am the one who has been blessed by having a good woman to go through life with.

It's also been my observation that nothing will divide siblings and make them combatants more quickly than a sudden infusion of money. Giving them a large inheritance increases the probability of tension and disharmony within a family. Sons and daughters often fight like cats and dogs over control of businesses, and they'll resent those who are designated as decision makers. And heaven help the in-laws who are put in positions of leadership. The green-eyed monsters of jealousy and resentment lurk in the shadows, ever threatening to destroy the closest of relationships.

World-famous British primatologist Jane Goodall produced a video some years ago that documented behavioral characteristics of chimpanzees. The troop lived in relative harmony most of the time. They lounged around grooming one another and watching their babies. Then the researchers dumped a huge pile of bananas in the area. It was like putting a match to gasoline. The chimps instantly became violent and vicious as they fought to get at the fruit. They were biting and screaming at those near the center of the pile. It was quite a spectacle. One large male crammed four bananas into his mouth sideways, distorting his face. Then he ran away carrying about a dozen more. He was followed by three other males who were trying to tear the bananas out of his hands. Clearly, the abundance of fruit had turned the peaceful chimps into warriors.[3]

It is always problematic to apply the findings of animal research to humans, but there are similarities between chimps and people in this instance. What the chimps were displaying has a name. It is called greed, and we have all experienced it. This emotion can turn nice people into those who hate. The Scriptures condemn that behavior. Indeed, one of the Ten Commandments is "Thou shall not covet…"

Here's another question you should consider: Do you as a parent really want to throw a large basket of bananas into the midst of your peaceful family?

I know my views on this subject are unconventional and many of my readers will disagree. I understand their sentiment. One of the reasons people work so hard is so their children won't have to. They love their kids so much they want to make things easier for them. Even so, giving abundantly to those who haven't sacrificed and struggled to achieve should be done with the greatest care, forethought, and prayer.

Let me be clear. I am not criticizing those who have been blessed with significant wealth, nor does the Scripture condemn them. Abraham, Lot, David, Solomon, and Boaz all had enormous wealth in their day. However, there are biblical guidelines to be followed. The Apostle Paul has been quoted as saying that money is the root of all evil. It isn't true. What he actually wrote is this, "For the love of money is a root of all kinds of evil. Some people, eager for money, have wandered from the faith and pierced themselves with many (sorrows)" (1Tim. 6:10).

Here is the crux of the matter: money is power, and power is inherently corrupting. Lord Acton said, "Power corrupts, and absolute power corrupts absolutely."[4] That is one of the most astute observations of human nature ever spoken. Those who get their hands on power, especially when they are young and immature, are sometimes destroyed by it.

Jesus spoke more about money than any other subject, and most of his teachings came in the form of warnings. He told a rich young ruler to sell everything he had and give it to the poor. Why was He so demanding of this man who was searching for truth? It was because Jesus perceived that money was the young man's god. He valued it even more than eternal life, and walked away from Jesus very sad (see Luke 18:22–23).

This will sound harsh, but it is what I believe to be true. If you mishandle the transfer of wealth to immature individuals who don't know how to handle it, you run the risk of damning them eternally. Whether you give them large trust funds or small gifts, you really should teach them how to use those resources wisely while you can. The Lord's work is usually underfunded, and our obligation is to give sacrificially to programs that feed the poor, care for orphans, teach our students, fund our churches and ministries, and spread the Gospel of Jesus Christ. Giving money lavishly to those who don't know how to share their possessions is always a mistake.

Let me return to the central theme of this book. The legacy of which I write is not about money. In fact, it is almost irrelevant to the central premise. The greatest endowment for your children and grandchildren can't be deposited in a bank. It can't be sold or traded or borrowed. It is an unshakable heritage of faith. It is the only gift that will stand the test of time. Everything else will fade away. Only by introducing your sons and daughters to Jesus Christ will you help them secure eternal life. How is that accomplished? By starting early and being intentional about the spiritual training of your children. It won't happen if left to chance. As we have seen, you also need to pray "without ceasing" for those you love (1 Thes. 5:17 NKJV). The appendices to this book provide specific "how to" information about handling this greatest of life's challenges.

I said it before but it bears repeating. Modeling is the best evangelistic tool you have as young mothers and fathers. You might not have lived long enough to know that little boys and girls are watching your every move. In time, they will comprehend what matters most to you and what, deep inside, you don't actually care about. Your mannerisms and your quirks and your anger and your pleasures and your language and your "toys" will be incorporated into their own way of thinking. What you say is important, but what you do is infinitely more powerful. If you say that Jesus is Lord of your life, but you don't have time for devotions as a family while you are playing golf four hours every Saturday, the contradiction will be observed.

I'll return to my godly father to illustrate how he transferred his beliefs to me. Through most of my childhood, he was an evangelist. He was not a perfect man, certainly, and he wasn't even at home much of the time. He traveled four to six weeks on each trip, leaving behind the wife he loved and needed—because he knew I needed her more. I can't describe fully the cost of that sacrifice for him. Nevertheless, when my father returned, he was ours, and some of my happiest days were spent hunting and fishing and playing tennis and building things with my six-foot-four dad.

Even so, this man's greatest contribution to my life was not represented by what he did for or with me; rather, it was the consistency of his Christian testimony. It made the most significant impact on me! He attempted to bring every area of his being into harmony with the Scriptures he loved so dearly. There in his home where faults and frailties were impossible to hide, I never once saw him deliberately compromise the principles in which he believed. Jesus Christ meant more to him than life itself.

We've been talking about money. Here is how Dad felt about it. During the wartime years when everything was in short supply, he would drive hundreds of miles in an old car to visit a church that had called him to preach. They were usually small congregations, especially in the early years. Travel expenses were high and the "offering" given to evangelists was usually pitiful. In order to reduce costs, he typically stayed in pastors' homes during ten-day meetings. It was difficult, but being there gave him a firsthand look at the financial needs of the ministers and their families. More than once I remember my dad coming home after such a trip to greet my mother and me with warm embraces. Sooner or later, Mom would get around to asking the big question, "How much did they pay you?"

He would smile sheepishly and say, "Well...uh."

She then said, "I know. You gave it away again, didn't you?"

Dad would reply, "Yeah, Honey, I felt like I should. You know, that pastor has four kids and their shoes have holes in them.

The oldest daughter doesn't even have a winter coat to wear to school, and I just couldn't leave there without helping them out. So I raised a 'love offering' for the pastor's family on the final Sunday night and contributed my check back to them."

Mom knew what that meant. Bills would come due without the money to pay for them. Yet to her credit, she would always smile and say, "If that's what God asked you to do, then you know it's okay with me."

Then the inevitable would happen. A few days later, our money would be exhausted. I can still recall Dad asking Mom and me to join him in the bedroom where we knelt in prayer. He always prayed first.

"Dear Lord, we come to You today with a small problem that You already know about. It concerns our shortage of money. You told us if we would be faithful to You in our good times, then You would stand by us in our hour of difficulty. We have tried to obey You and to share our resources with others; now my little family is the one in need. We ask You to help us especially at this time."

I was only nine years old, but I was listening carefully to what my father said to God in those moments. You can also be assured that I was waiting to see what the Lord would do in response, and I was never disappointed. I tell you truthfully that money always came from unexpected sources in time to meet our need. On one occasion that is still vivid in my memory, a $1,200 check arrived in the mail the day after our humble family prayer. My faith grew by leaps and bounds as I watched my parents practicing the scriptural principles on which their very lives were founded.

It is also true that my mother and father were not able to accumulate a nest egg during their working years, and I was concerned about them as they grew older. I worried about how they would pay for medical expenses and related obligations in their retirement years. I think my mother was worried about that, too. Women do tend to fret about things like that.

One day long after I was a man, my parents were scheduled to go out to dinner with friends. As usual, Dad got ready first. He was lying on the bed while Mom combed her hair. As she turned to look at him she noticed that he had tears in his eyes.

"What's the matter?" she asked.

He hesitated and then said, "The Lord just spoke to me."

"Do you want to tell me about it?" she asked.

"He told me something about you," said my father.

"Then you'd better tell me!" insisted Mom.

"Well, I was just lying here thinking," he said. "I wasn't even praying, but the Lord promised me that He was going to take care of you."

They wondered what the strange revelation could have meant and then went on with their evening plans. In my final telephone conversation with my dad, he told me this story. Five days later, my father suffered a massive heart attack from which he never recovered.

Being an only son, I was responsible for my mother's financial affairs after my dad's passing. I was alarmed to see that after the sale of her house and redeeming a couple of small life insurance policies, she only had $46,000 to take with her into the future. The church denomination in which my father had served for forty-two years offered almost nothing in the way of retirement benefit for its older ministers. The church had millions of dollars in its preachers' benevolent fund, but the leadership provided my mother with a paltry $58 per month—barely enough to keep gasoline in her car. Other men who pastored small churches that couldn't even make Social Security payments were hard-pressed to survive. It was disgraceful. If I hadn't been able to help provide for Mom financially, she could have been stuck in county facilities for the rest of her life.

Six years passed and Mom contracted Parkinson's disease. She was hospitalized permanently. Her condition worsened and she required more and more care, eventually needing skilled nursing supervision twenty-four hours a day. Even in the late 1980s, the expense was in excess of $50,000 per year. Here's the miraculous part of the story: Right on schedule, the value of the Coca-Cola stock Dad had inherited from his father almost fifty years earlier began to rise in value. Mom lived five more years before dying in 1988, and would you believe, I never gave her a cent because she didn't need it. The Lord kept His promise. He took care of Myrtle Dobson until the day He called her home.

By the way, bequeathing money to offspring doesn't *have to be* a negative thing. It all depends on the need and the preparation made for it.

I had watched the life and times of my parents as the years unfolded through my young eyes. The faith that I learned at their knees is still vibrant, and it lives today within the hearts and minds of our grown children. God is faithful! And He keeps His word.

—∿—

I can't close this book without sharing a passage in Scripture that puts our entire discussion into perspective. It is reported

in 1 Chronicles 28, when King David had grown old and knew
he was dying. He called together his officials, military leaders,
business managers, and "mighty men" to hear his final words.
In the assembly that day was his son Solomon, whom God had
chosen to succeed David as king. A very touching and historic
conversation then occurred between the dying monarch and
his young heir.

The advice David gave that day was of great significance,
not only for Solomon but also for you and me. A person doesn't
waste words when the death angel hovers nearby. Picture
the scene, then, as the old man offers his last thoughts to his
beloved son, who would carry on his legacy. This is what David
said, probably with strong feeling and a shaky voice:

> And you, my son Solomon, acknowledge the God of your
> father, and serve him with wholehearted devotion and
> with a willing mind, for the Lord searches every heart and
> understands every desire and every thought. If you seek
> him, he will be found by you; but if you forsake him, he
> will reject you forever. (1 Chron. 28:9)

A lifetime of wisdom was packed into that brief statement
from the godly king. Notice first that David advised Solomon
to "know" God. He didn't say "know *about* God." I know about
Abraham Lincoln, but I've never met him. David wanted Solomon to be acquainted personally with the God of Abraham,
Isacc, and Jacob, whom he had tried to serve with a willing mind.

It is also my best advice to you as we conclude these thoughts
about *Your Legacy*. Advise your sons and daughters, above all
else, to get to know God and seek His will for their lives. If
they make that their priority, they *will* find Him. Jesus Christ

will lead them. He will bless them. What a wonderful promise! But it is conditional. If they turn their backs on the Lord, He will cast them off forever. You owe it to your children to emphasize that sobering warning as well.

—⁓—

In conclusion, I ask parents again: What will be your legacy on behalf of those you love? Will you help them build a foundation of faith that will sustain them through the trials of life and take them into the better world beyond? Will they be there to greet you and the rest of your family and Christian friends on the other side? That is my prayer for you.

A day of celebration is coming like nothing that has ever occurred in the history of mankind. The Guest of Honor on that morning will be One wearing a seamless robe, with eyes like flames of fire and feet like fine brass. As we bow humbly before Him, we will hear a great voice out of heaven saying:

Now the dwelling place of God is with men, and he will live with them. They will be his people, and God himself will be with them and be their God. He will wipe every tear from their eyes. There will be no more death or mourning or crying or pain, for the old order of things has passed away. (Rev. 21:3–4)

And, again the mighty voice will echo through the corridors of time:

Never again will they hunger; never again will they thirst. The sun will not beat upon them, nor any scorching heat. For the Lamb at the center of the throne will be their shepherd; he will lead them to springs of living water. And God will wipe away every tear from their eyes. (Rev. 7:16–17)

This is the hope of the ages that burns within my breast. It is the ultimate answer to those who suffer and struggle today. It is the only solace for those who have said good-bye to a loved one. Though the pain is indescribable now, we must never forget that our separation is temporary. If our children and loved ones have given their hearts to the Lord, we will be reunited forever on that glad resurrection morning. As the Scripture promises, our tears will be banished forever!

I'll meet my great-grandfather George Washington McCluskey for the first time, and see my great-grandmother, Nanny. Big Mama and Little Daddy will be there, too, standing beside Robert Dobson and Little Mother. Shirley's stepfather and mother, Joe and Alma, will be on hand. My mother and father will also be there. My dad will be straining to catch a glimpse of our arrival, just as he and Mom did for so many Christmas seasons when Shirley and I flew with our children into the Kansas City airport. They will have so much to tell us that they'll be bursting with excitement. Mom often complained that Dad would want to hustle me off to some distant planet he's discovered while exploring the universe. Your children and loved ones who died in Christ will also be in that great throng, singing and shouting the praises of the Redeemer. What a celebration it will be!

This is the reward for the faithful. This is the crown of righteousness prepared for those who have fought a good fight, finished the course, and kept the faith (2 Tim. 4:7–8). Throughout our remaining days in this life, therefore, let me urge you not to be discouraged by temporal cares. Accept the circumstances as they are presented to you. Give the highest priority to the spiritual training of your sons and daughters. They deserve your best.

I will leave you with a sweet little poem that I have loved for many years. It was written by Florence Jones Hadley, who would have understood what I have written.

Are All the Children In?

I think at times as the night draws nigh
Of an old house on the hill,
And of a yard all wide and blossomed-starred
Where the children play at will.
And when the night at last came down
Hushing the merry din',
Mother would look around and ask,
"Are all the children in?"

Oh, it's many, many a year since then,
And the old house on the hill
No longer echoes to childish feet
And the yard is still, so still.

But I see it all, as the shadows creep,
And though many the years since then
I can still hear my mother ask,
"Are all the children in?"

I wonder if when the shadows fall
On our last short earthly day

When we say good-bye to the world outside,
All tired with our childish play,
When we step out into the other Land
Where mother so long has been,
Will we hear her ask, just as of old,
"Are all the children in?"[5]

—⁂—

The last word: Give your children and loved ones a simple but profound message as you prepare to step into the next world, "BE THERE!" If you accomplish that purpose, it will be your greatest legacy.

APPENDICES

Many parents have asked for some very practical help with the spiritual training of their children. I have turned to two experts, Robert and Bobbie Wolgemuth, who have worked extensively with boys and girls. Bobbie especially is a "guru" with little people and she has a wonderful singing voice. In their book, How to Lead Your Child to Christ,[1] *Robert and Bobbie crafted some ideas, stories, and explanations to help moms and dads teach basic Christian concepts at home. I've included some of them in the two appendices that follow. I appreciate Robert's and Bobbie's thoughtful assistance in this project.*

APPENDIX 1

Strategies to Build Your Legacy

Studies show that the great majority of people who accept Jesus as their Lord and Savior do so as children. So creating a spiritual climate in your home that can help nurture your child's faith is your most important assignment. Here are some strategies that can help insure that your child will be ready to accept God's gift of grace when the time is right.

Bibles for Everyone

If you've not already done so, consider buying a Bible for everyone in your family, including the youngest children.

Before you tuck your children into bed at night, read from *their* Bible. If they're old enough, encourage them to read along.

God promises that His Word will provide a lifetime of light for your children's path...a cure for their lifelong struggle with sin.

How can a young man cleanse his way?
By taking heed according to Your word.
With my whole heart I have sought You;
Oh, let me not wander from Your commandments!
Your word I have hidden in my heart,
That I might not sin against You...
Your word is a lamp to my feet and a light to my path.

(Ps. 119: 9–11, 105 NKJV)

The path to obedience is paved with God's Word.

Memorizing Scripture

One way to help pass on your spiritual legacy to your children is to help them memorize important Scripture verses. Their brains are like wet cement, and the verses they learn will be pressed on their hearts forever.

An easy way to help them memorize a passage is to write a version out on an index card and then look for chances to repeat it, phrase by phrase, to your kids. Riding in the car on the way to school or sitting around the breakfast table are perfect chances for you to work on your verse together. You can even turn the process into a game. A great verse to start with is Philippians 4:13: "I can do all things through Christ who strengthens me" (NKJV).

When kids are struggling with doubt or temptation, the Holy Spirit can use His own words, which they've memorized, to strengthen their faith and resolve.

Teach Them to Pray

Bringing your children into God's presence through prayer is an unspeakable privilege. Teaching them to pray also gives you the opportunity to show them another way to honor the Lord.

Mealtimes and bedtimes are ideal times for prayer. By your own example, teach your child how to speak words of affirmation and gratitude to God. The younger your child, the more likely he is to thank God for unusual things, like the frog in the creek or a new box of breakfast cereal. That's okay—the older he gets, the more meaningful these thank-yous will become.

Also teach your child to learn to ask forgiveness for specific actions. By confessing his own sin, your child will begin to understand the truth of a loving heavenly Father's forgiveness.

Then invite your child to bring his requests to the God of the universe, who is listening carefully. Like his list of thank-yous, he may have a long list of everyday requests ("Bless the garbage man, bless my Hot Wheels and Rescue Heroes, please help my T-ball team win tomorrow…"). Again, it's okay. Your child is learning to trust God to meet his needs.

Finally, help your child close the prayer by thanking God once more.

The best way for your child to learn how to pray is for them to hear you pray with them and for them. Let them hear you speak words of adoration and worship, confess your sins, make specific requests, and then thank Him again for listening and answering.

Table Talk

So much of passing along your legacy to your children will be found in the ordinary moments...such as engaging in conversation around the dinner table.

One way to initiate good conversation is to ask two questions: "What was the happiest thing that happened today?" and "Did you have any sad moments today?" This always evokes interesting family talk. This is a good way to get the kids involved in the discussion.

Another way of focusing family talk with your kids is to ask them, "Did the Lord say anything special to you today?" This is a *great* idea. Help your children learn to keep their eyes and ears tuned for God's activity in their lives during the day, anticipating the time they could give a report to their family at dinner.

Sing Together

For thousands of years, Christ-followers have celebrated their friendship with God through the singing of hymns and spiritual songs. Profound lyrics set to beautiful melodies have provided instruction, comfort, and hope to millions of believers around the world for centuries. They're also a great way for you to teach your children the truths of the Christian faith.

And, of course, every Sunday morning we affirm with other believers our faith in Jesus Christ through the singing of hymns and praise songs. Singing together has played a vital role in the Christian faith, and music is a natural way for you to teach your children sound theology.

After your family sings a hymn together just two or three times, you'll be surprised at how quickly your children will have them memorized. Soon you'll hear them singing the words to themselves. You'll know that the words are sinking in their heart and building their character. Imagine the pure delight of passing the love of hymns to your children and then, in turn, to their children. Can you imagine the fun of hearing your two-year-old grandchild singing as she washes her hands, "What can wash away my sin? Nothing but the blood of Jesus."

Connect with a Local Church

Another way you can teach your children to love and honor Christ is by taking them to church every week. There's a kind of ecstasy about sitting together as a family and worshipping the God you love. Your child hears your voice singing and praying and it creates a bond with Christ, His family, and with you.

Church is the place where you and your children can gain a deeper knowledge of God's Word in Sunday school and small group Bible studies. When they're older, your children may sign up for a mission trip where God's work across the world can be brought into sharp focus.

Your church is filled with other adults with whom your children will establish friendships. During those times when you and your children aren't connecting as well as you should, these "free adults" will affirm what you have taught your kids. They'll help to keep them solidly grounded in their walk with Christ.

Like "home base" when you were young and played hide-and-seek, your church is a safe place—a fortress, really—that has stood firm against centuries of all kinds of warfare—visible and invisible.

Jesus said, "I will build my church, and all the powers of hell will not conquer it" (Matt. 16:18 NLT).

That sounds like a good place for you and your children to hang out, doesn't it?

Passing on Your Faith

The best way to begin a conversation about your child's need to receive the gift of God's grace is to tell them about your own journey of faith. You can also remind them:

- How great and good their Heavenly Father is…how dearly He loves them;
- How much they need Jesus to forgive them for things they do that displease Him;
- How Jesus's death on the cross and resurrection from the grave saves them from their sin and Satan's power over them and brings them into a lifelong friendship with God; and
- That God loves them so much that He wants to live in their hearts and take them to heaven when they die.

Praying to Receive Christ

Though we cannot accept salvation *for* our children, we can help them understand how to grab hold of salvation once they recognize their need for Christ and express their desire to come to Him. Some parents take their children through this step by praying with them something like this:

Dear Heavenly Father. Thank you for loving me. I know that I am a sinful boy and need you to save me. Thank you for sending your Son to die on the cross for me and for raising Him from the dead. I receive your gift of forgiveness; thank you for your promise to live in my heart for the rest of my life. And thank you for listening to me when I talk to you and for the promise that you will take me to heaven when I die. Amen.

Whether you help them with the words or give them enough information so they can come to Christ with their own prayer, the important thing is that they sincerely speak words of gratitude, repentance, acknowledgment of God's grace, and acceptance and thanks for His promises.

Celebrate Your Child's Decision

If salvation is important enough to God that He asks His angels to throw a party, you can do the same. Consider celebrating when your child comes to Jesus…by making a phone call to tell grandparents or a special Christian friend; buying a new Bible and writing your child's name and "new birth date" in the front. You may want to let your child choose a special place for dinner—or his favorite meal at home. These are ways to make the experience memorable, setting it apart like you do the child's physical birthday.

Like the angels did when the shepherd found his lost sheep, the woman found her lost coin, and the waiting father welcomed his lost son, you can rejoice because the *lost* has been *found*. That's reason enough to celebrate!

APPENDIX 2

Stories to Build Your Legacy

Research has shown that the single most important thing a parent can do to help his or her child acquire language, prepare them for school, and instill in them a love of learning is teaching them to read. Here are ten stories you can read aloud to your children to help them to better understand what it means for Christ to be their Savior and Friend.

One Girl's Story

My name is Mrs. Wolgemuth. You can call me Miss Bobbie, as the kids in our neighborhood call me. I am a grandmother with grandchildren like you, and I know a little girl who has asked me to tell you her story but would like to keep her name a secret. You can be sure that every bit of her story is true, because she wanted you to know just what happened when she was only eight years old.

Let me start by telling you that this little girl had everything most children would ever dream of owning. Her daddy was a wealthy doctor and often brought home wonderful gifts and toys for his daughter. And her mother was a beautiful woman who wore fancy clothes and lovely jewelry. This girl lived in a big redbrick house and went swimming, played tennis, or rode her bike whenever she liked. A very proper English nanny took care of the girl and her sisters during the week while their mother was out attending tea parties, fashion shows, and other special events. On Sundays, everyone in the family slept late except her dad, who played golf at the country club nearby.

Most people would say the hazel-eyed youngster was a nice enough girl, with a lot of talent. She took piano lessons and enjoyed playing for her mother's friends. And, even though she had what most people would call a very nice life, this little girl told me that she often felt very empty on the inside. Sometimes she even thought about doing mean things when no one was watching, like the day at school she decided to use really wicked words, yelling some hurtful things to a classmate when the teacher wasn't listening. Yes, this girl told me that she acted sweet and kind in front of grown-ups, but on the inside she had hateful, ugly feelings and was very selfish.

One of the best things this girl remembers about her life as a kid is that a family of angels lived across the street from her house. I say angels, because that is what the girl herself called them. Their real names were Mr. and Mrs. Lay—Homer and Libby. They had a daughter named Martha, who the girl says was the brightest angel of all. Why, even when faced with this spoiled little neighbor, Martha would be kind and played with her. Even though Martha did not have as many toys or fancy clothes as her neighbor, there *was* something Martha had that made the little girl want to go to Martha's house whenever she could. Do you want to know what it was?

Well, there was so much love at Martha's home that it touched everyone who walked in the door. Her mother usually greeted the neighborhood kids with a smile, a hug, and a "Welcome children; please come inside." Then Mrs. Lay would sit with the neighborhood kids and talk and ask questions about the children's day. Sometimes she would let them hold the new baby named Ann. Near the end of most visits, everyone would go over to the brown piano in the corner of the playroom and sing some special songs.

The girl who told me the story said that at night when she was alone in bed, she would think about the family across the street. Why did she feel so special there? She wondered what made Martha's family so different from her own. She thought about the words to the songs she had sung at their house. There was something about those songs that made her feel happy inside, as if an angel had come to visit her.

The little girl asked Martha about the wonderful feeling at her house, and Martha told the girl that it was because Somebody very special lived at her house. His name was Jesus.

The little girl wondered why Jesus had come to Martha's house but not to hers. She wished that He would come to live at her house, too. The little girl remembered that her grandmother had taught her to pray, so at night she said her prayers and hoped that angels would visit her home while she slept.

Every Sunday morning Martha's family climbed into their car, and off they went to church. One Sunday, the little girl and her sisters were invited to go along. Excited as little butterflies, the girls put on their prettiest dresses and scrunched into the backseat next to Martha to go along. *Maybe this will be the place to find out about Jesus*, the little girl hoped.

Inside the church building, everyone stood to sing like one huge choir. The sound was so wonderful that the little girl thought she must be in heaven. In Sunday school, she listened to the teacher and decided for sure that Jesus lived there in that church, too. *But how could she take Him home with her? How could she tell her mom and dad about the angels?*

Later that day, back in the neighborhood, Mrs. Lay sat on the porch with the little girl and her sisters. "I am glad you liked church," she said with a smile. "What was your favorite part?"

"Well, my teacher hugged me and gave me my very own Bible," said the little girl. "And she said that Jesus can live in your heart. But I don't know if He wants to come into *my* heart."

The girl asked a lot of questions until finally Mrs. Lay said, "Would you like to invite Jesus to live in your heart? If you ask Him to come in, you can be sure that He will. He wants to help you grow into the person He created you to be. I will pray with you if you'd like."

The little girl spoke right up, "Oh, I'd like that very much. But what about all the hateful, ugly things I've said and done?"

"That is exactly why Jesus died on the cross," said Mrs. Lay. "All of us have ugly things in our hearts that need to be forgiven. Jesus makes you a brand-new person on the inside. Then He helps you to obey Him."

At that moment, the angels must have been swirling all around the neighborhood, for the little girl *did* pray and ask Jesus to forgive her. She didn't wait another minute. She asked Him to come and live in her heart and make her home like Martha's.

Something happened that made the girl feel very happy. She would tell you that she still wasn't perfect after that, but she *did* have a new best friend named Jesus to help her. She read her new Bible and tried to learn as much as she could. That very day, the little girl took Jesus home with her, and everyone soon noticed that she was happier and kinder than she had ever been. Every day she knelt down next to her bed and prayed that Jesus would fill her heart and her home with His love. And He did.

The girl wants you to know that Jesus can live in your house, too. He is the best friend to have, because He is with you all the time. He helps you do what is kind and loving, just as if He lived right inside your heart, and He can change your whole family. The girl who told me the story hopes that you will pray and ask Jesus to forgive your sins and come to live in your heart…and in your home, too. She also hopes that you will pray for your family and for the kids in your neighborhood. And the girl said she's glad that now you know her story.

By the way, if you are wondering how I know so much about this girl, I think it's time to tell you. You see, I'm a grandmother now, but I was that little girl a long time ago.

Miss Bobbie

One Boy's Story

My name is Luke and I am six years old. Not long ago my family celebrated a special day for my brother, Isaac, and I want to tell you about it.

Isaac is four years old and goes to preschool two days a week. One day his teacher asked the children to make cutout letters of the alphabet at home and bring them to school for a project. I watched my mom help Isaac cut out his letters at the kitchen table. For each letter, Isaac thought of a word that begins with that letter. When they got to the letter *J*, Isaac said, "*J* is for Jesus."

"That's good, Isaac," my mom said. "Someday I hope you will invite Jesus to live in your heart."

Isaac was quiet for a minute. Then he said, "I want to invite Jesus into my heart today, Mom."

My mom asked Isaac if he knew what it meant to invite Jesus into his heart. He said that he wasn't sure, so she picked up some pieces of colored construction paper to explain it. She chose five colors: gold, black, red, white, and green. I will tell you what each color means.

Gold stands for God and for heaven, God's home. The Bible says that in heaven the streets are made of gold and no one is sick there and no one ever dies. God is holy and perfect and made heaven and earth. And God made you and me. He loves us and wants us to live with Him in heaven someday.

Black is like the darkness of sin. Sin is anything that makes God sad—things I think about or do that hurt others, like being selfish or hitting my sister. It's sin in my heart that makes me tell lies and say mean things. The Bible says everyone sins. My sins keep me away from God. But God loves me even when I do bad things. And He wants to give me a clean, new heart that doesn't have sin in it.

Red stands for Jesus' blood. God sent His Son, Jesus, to be punished for my sin. Jesus died on a cross, but on the third day, God raised Him to life again.

White is the color of snow, and that's how clean my heart can be. I need to tell Jesus that I am sorry for my sin and believe that He died for me.

Green is the color of grass and trees and things that grow. It reminds me that I need to grow to love God more and more. After I ask Jesus to forgive my sin, my love for God can grow strong. I can keep growing by learning about God in the Bible and going to church and praying.

When Isaac asked Jesus to come into his heart, he prayed a special prayer. My mom said a few words and then let Isaac repeat them. I remember praying like that when I invited Jesus into my heart. This is the prayer that my mom helped Isaac to pray:

"Dear God, thank You for loving me so much. Thank You for sending Jesus to die for me and take my sin away. I know I have sin in my heart. Please forgive my sin. I want to make You happy. I want my heart to be as clean and white as snow. Please come into my heart and help me love You more every day. Amen."

Because Isaac invited Jesus into his heart, we had a family celebration. This was just like we did when my sister and I invited Jesus to come into our hearts. Everyone in my family makes a big deal about it because Dad and Mom say it's like a birthday. The person gets to pick what they want for dinner. I chose pizza—without mushrooms—on my special day, and Isaac said he wanted to go out for a cheeseburger. We call our Grammie and Papa and Granddaddy and Nanny on the phone and later we buy a new Bible.

Now everyone in my family is a Christian. Sometimes at dinner my dad asks us, "What did God say to you today?" and we each say what we think God said to us in our heart. One day I had a new set of LEGOs. All day long I thought about those LEGOs. When it was my turn to answer my dad's question, I told everyone, "God wants me to love Jesus more than my LEGOs."

God is always helping me to make wise choices and to love Him more than anything else. He can help you, too.

Who Made Thunderstorms?

What do you do during thunderstorms, the kind of rumbling storms that light up the sky and rattle the windows? *Boom! Boom! Boom!* goes the thunder. It sounds like gunshots right outside your home. The lightning flashes like fireworks.

Once there were some kids who came up with a plan to keep from being scared by thunderstorms. When the thunderstorm starts to roll in, they all huddle together wherever they are—on the sofa or on the biggest bed in the house—and "snuggle" until the storm is over. At the first sounds of the frightful noises and sights, someone says, "Oh, goodie, it's time to snuggle!" Then everyone runs to the circle of hugs. All of the kids have a hand to hold and someone to be close to as they watch and listen to the storm outside.

The Bible tells us who made the skies where the storms come from. God made them. God is the One who created everything in the heavens and on the earth. He is the Lord God Almighty, the Maker of heaven and earth. The Bible says that God sends out His mighty voice and that His power is in the skies (see Ps. 68:33). And like our friends who snuggle during the thunderstorms, God also gently holds us with His love (see Deut. 33: 26–27). What an awesome God He is!

God lives in heaven, and besides being very powerful, He is also perfect. There is one word that means "perfect." All the angels in heaven use it over and over again as they sing about God. They say "Holy! Holy! Holy!" and they do everything God tells them to do. God wants you and me to know how great and kind He is. He wants us to reverence Him, too. That means to show respect for Him and obey Him because of how perfect and mighty and kind He is.

There is a very special hymn that helps us to sing about our perfect and wonderful God. When we sing "Holy! Holy! Holy!" we use the same word the angels do to tell God how mighty He is.

We can talk to God out loud or silently in our hearts and tell Him that He is powerful and mighty and perfect. We can thank Him for all He has made and remember that He loves us. It's sort of like running to your dad or mom in a storm. When you talk to God about His love for you and your love for Him, it's like you're snuggling with Him. He wants you to know that He is strong and can keep you safe.

The next time you hear thunder or see a flash of lightning or look at the beautiful sky after the storm, remember the Lord God Almighty who created it all. Remember that He is holy and that He loves you very much.

The Gift of Life

Did you know that there is over a gallon of blood inside your body? That's a lot. Of course, you and I don't think about our blood because we can't see it…that is, unless we fall and scrape our knee. We put a Band-Aid on the tender place until it heals.

Blood carries good things—called oxygen and nutrients—inside our body to keep us healthy. Sometimes people get very sick because their blood is weak. They need good blood to help them get well. But where can they get this good blood?

Often near a hospital there is a building with a large red cross painted on the wall. It's a place where people can give some of their blood so it can be used for sick patients. (Don't worry. When people give blood, their body makes more.)

People walking by the Red Cross building may see a big sign that says "Give Someone the Gift of Life." The hospital wants everyone to know that people who have been hurt or who are very sick need some good blood. Only blood that is clean and free from disease can be put into the patients at the hospital. With new, healthy blood, a sick person's body can fight off illness and get better.

Though most people have healthy blood, everyone's heart is filled with sin. It's as if our heart is sick. Our heart is the part of us that thinks and feels and decides to do right or wrong. The Bible says, "All have sinned and fall short of the glory of God" (Rom. 3:23). So everyone needs some powerful healing blood to make their heart clean and healthy and forgiven by God.

There is a wonderful song that asks the question, "What Can Wash Away My Sin?" The answer the song gives is, "Nothing but the blood of Jesus." When Jesus died on the cross, He gave His perfect blood to make everyone clean from sin. The Bible says, "Without the shedding of blood there is no forgiveness" (Heb. 9:22).

Do you remember the sign at the Red Cross that said, "Give Someone the Gift of Life"? Jesus is the only One who can forgive our sin and give the gift of *eternal* life. He gives it to every person who believes in Him. Jesus said, "I have come that they may have life, and that they may have it more abundantly" (John 10:10 NKJV). He gave His blood on the cross to make us new and keep us strong enough to follow Him even when it's hard.

Because Jesus came back to life after He died on the cross, we will come back to life after we die, too. Then we will live with Him in heaven. This is the gift of eternal life. Jesus said, "My sheep listen to my voice; I know them, and they follow me. I give them eternal life, and they shall never perish; no one can snatch them out of my hand" (John 10:27–28). You can be sure that you have eternal life when you believe Jesus and ask

Him to wash your heart clean with His perfect blood. And He will never leave you.

The next time you see a cross on a building, on jewelry, or anywhere else, remember that Jesus is the only one who can give the gift of everlasting life. The song "What Can Wash Away My Sin?" tells the truth. Just like the hospital knows that you need good blood to live on this earth, God knows that nothing but the blood of Jesus can make it possible for us to live forever in heaven.

The Happiest Day Ever

Jesus knew that He had important work to do for God, His Father in heaven. He knew that He was going to die for the sins of all the people in the world so they would be able to live with God someday. That was hard for His friends to understand, so He kept telling them not to be afraid, but to trust Him. He said, "Let not your hearts be troubled. Believe in God; believe also in Me" (John 14:1 ESV).

Jesus also told His friends that after He died He would not stay dead. He knew He would come to life again. He said anyone who believes in Him will also live again in heaven. He didn't want His friends to worry. Jesus said, "I will not leave you as orphans; I will come to you. Before long, the world will not see me anymore, but you will see me. Because I live, you also will live" (John 14:18–19).

After Jesus died on the cross, His body was laid in a grave. It was like a cave inside a big rock and it was called a tomb. The disciples were very sad that their best friend, Jesus, had died. They forgot that Jesus had said He would come back to life. That's probably because they didn't understand, so they didn't really believe Him. When a body is dead, it doesn't look like it could ever live again.

But Jesus did come back to life. That was called Jesus' resurrection, and it was the happiest day ever! It happened on a Sunday morning long ago. The ground trembled with a force greater than a mighty earthquake. Jesus walked right out of the grave, alive! A dazzling angel told some of His friends not to worry. The angel said, "Do not be afraid, for I know that you seek Jesus who was crucified. He is not here, for He has risen, as He said" (Matt. 28:5–6 ESV).

Most of Jesus' close friends were meeting together in a house on that Sunday. In the evening Jesus surprised them and walked right into the room. He stood there, showing His friends that He was alive! They couldn't believe it. Jesus told them to look at His hands and feet so they would know it was really Him. He ate some food so they'd know He wasn't a ghost. He was real, and He was really alive!

Everyone began telling their friends about the Resurrection. That's how the Christian faith started spreading all over the world. Before Jesus went back to heaven, He told His friends to keep letting people know that He was alive and would never leave them. He said, "Go and make disciples of all nations, baptizing them in the name of the Father and of the Son and of the Holy Spirit, and teaching them to obey everything I have commanded you. And surely I am with you always, to the very end of the age" (Matt. 28:19–20).

Sunday, the first day of the week, is the day when Jesus came back to life. That's why so many churches hold services on Sundays. We go to celebrate Jesus' resurrection. Jesus lives. That's why we read the Bible and pray in Jesus' name. We know He is alive and hears us.

We can tell our friends about God's mighty power and the Resurrection. We can tell them that they can live forever in heaven with Jesus.

Yes, it was the happiest day ever when Jesus came to life again!

Lost and Found

Have you ever been lost and unsure what to do? It's extremely sad to be lost. Once there was a little boy who was standing near a checkout counter surrounded by a crowd of busy shoppers. He had dark brown hair and looked to be about five years old. Big tears rolled down his face as he stood on his tiptoes searching for his mother. He couldn't see her anywhere. No longer trying to act brave, the boy started sobbing so loudly that several shoppers took notice and bent down to talk to him.

"What's your name?" one kind lady asked. Of course he knew his name, but the boy was crying so hard he couldn't speak. He was lost and didn't know what to do.

Just then, the boy's mom pushed her way through the crowd saying, "Oh, there you are! I was looking for you, Conner! I've been looking everywhere for you." Conner squeezed his arms tightly around his mom's neck as she hugged him close. A big smile came across his face. And it didn't take any time to wipe away Conner's tears after that big hug.

Then Conner took his mom's hand, and they walked through the busy store together. The little boy was so happy to be with his mom that he decided he would hold her hand and not wander off again to see anything, no matter how interesting it looked. He would stay right next to his mom and make sure he followed her everywhere she went.

Jesus is a lot like the mom who came to find Conner. Jesus loves His children and doesn't want them to be lost. He wants His children near Him all day and all night. He came looking for you to tell you that He loves you and wants you to stay close to Him in your heart. You can make up your mind to hold on to every word He says in the Bible. You can decide to follow Him every day by believing that He is God's Son and by doing what pleases God. With God's words in your heart, you will remember what to do, how to act, and what to say.

Getting to Know Your New Friend

When you meet new friends, how do you get to know them? The best way is to spend time with them. If a new friend wrote you a letter, you would read it over and over and think about it, wouldn't you? When you invite Jesus to be your new friend, you'll want to learn all about Him. You'll want to have your very own Bible, a wonderful letter from God that will help you get to know who God is and what He likes.

The Bible explains everything about God and His Son, Jesus. It tells you that He created the world and lets you know why He made you and how much He loves you. The Bible teaches what is right and tells how to stay away from things that make God unhappy.

There are many books in the Bible—sixty-six of them! It's divided into two sections: the Old Testament and the New Testament. Some books tell you stories about people. There were many people who lived for God and did great things. But some people did not live to please God, and their stories are very sad. Other books are filled with poetry, songs, prayers, and instructions from God. Still others contain special messages from God to His people. The stories about Jesus, your new friend, begin in the New Testament.

Since you want to get to know God, you can study the Bible a little each day. You may choose to start by reading the Gospel of John.

Whenever you read a paragraph or verse in the Bible, it helps if you do two things: (1) ask God to help you understand His letter to you; (2) stop and think about what you have just read.

Sometimes it helps to ask yourself two questions that begin with *What*: (1) "What does this say?" and (2) "What does it mean to me?" This is how you hear God's voice. It's good to think about the words a few minutes after you read them. You can ask God to speak to you in your heart through the words you have read.

There are beautiful songs that keep God's words rolling over and over in your mind. These words will help you remember and want to do what God tells you to do. You'll like the song "Trust and Obey." It's fun to sing about being "happy in Jesus."

As you read your Bible and sing the songs you've learned, you will notice that you have a very happy feeling inside your heart. That's because you're spending time with your friend, the Lord Jesus. He knows how to make you happy. His Holy Spirit lives in your heart and will remind you that He loves you. He will give you ideas of things you can do that please God. He will help you to say no to things that are harmful and wrong, and yes to things that are good and right. You will enjoy a wonderful friendship and a great adventure as you learn to trust and obey God. That's something to smile about. What a great friend you have!

Growing in God's Garden

Have you ever planted a seed and watched it turn into a big green plant? It takes a lot of sunshine and water for the seed to grow. Pretty soon a tiny stem appears, and after a while green leaves pop out. The leaves point up toward the sun to grow even stronger. The roots grow down deeper and deeper to drink water. The next thing you know, you see a beautiful flower, a healthy vegetable, or a yummy fruit. If you've ever eaten a sweet grape or a crunchy apple, remember that it started as a tiny little seed.

When your friendship with Jesus grows, you're like that little seed. After you prayed and asked Jesus to forgive your sins, it was like you were planted in God's garden. Now, little by little, you will grow to be a strong follower of Jesus. This will happen as you read or listen to God's Word and learn to know Him better. You will grow as you go to church and Sunday school. That's where you learn about Jesus Christ and meet with other people who are following Him. You will grow when you give some of your money to your church. You will grow when you sing songs that keep thoughts about God in your mind. You will grow every time you pray and thank God for good food to eat. You will even grow at night when you say your prayers. Before you go to sleep is a great time to think about a Bible verse or the words to a hymn. And you can ask the Lord to be with you all night while you are sleeping.

One of the wonderful things God wants you to do after you become a Christian is to grow like a strong plant that produces good fruit. When you read the Bible, pray, go to church, give your money, and sing songs that fill your mind with the sunshine of God's love, good things will happen. The Bible says that love, joy, peace, patience, kindness, goodness, faithfulness, gentleness, and self-control are like fruit that grows if you love Jesus and let God's Spirit live in you (Gal. 5:22–23). When other people see you bursting with good fruit like this, they will know you have asked the Lord Jesus to help you grow in His garden.

And there's something else that happens when you grow. Every time you tell your friends about the love of Jesus, you will be planting seeds that may grow into new Christians. That's the most fun of all. If you see a friend or someone in your family with a little seed of faith, it will make you very happy to see that person grow to love Jesus more and more. You'll feel so happy that you will jump up and down. That's how God plans for His garden to grow. He is happy, too, when your family and friends grow into strong followers of His Son, Jesus.

Jesus wants you to grow close to Him. To make sure that happens, be sure to stay in the sunshine of God's love—read your Bible, pray every day, go to church, be generous with your money, sing songs of praise to God, and tell others about His wonderful love. The more you grow to be like God's Son, Jesus, the more great things you'll be able to do for God.

Being on God's Team

Have you ever been to a ball game and listened as everyone shouted for his or her team? The fans say special cheers together like "We've got spirit, yes we do, we've got spirit, how about you?" Everyone is encouraged to be winners when they cheer together.

Jesus and His followers are a team. The first Christians needed something like a cheer that they could say. It would help them remember that they were all on the same team. It would also help them remember what they believed. They call their cheer the Apostles' Creed. It was called a creed because the word *creed* means "I believe."

The twelve men who were Jesus' disciples are also called apostles. That means they were with Jesus while He lived on earth, and they followed Him. Even though you and I have not actually seen Jesus, we know that He is with us because He says in the Bible that He will always be with us. When we have asked Jesus to come and live in our hearts, we are like the apostles. We follow Jesus by obeying Him and following what He teaches us in the Bible. Because we follow Jesus, we can "listen" to His voice speaking in our heart.

During worship services, Christians all around the world say the Apostles' Creed together as a reminder of what all of us believe about God, about Jesus, and about the Holy Spirit. It makes us feel strong to be able to speak what we believe. Saying the Apostles' Creed also makes us feel close to Christians in other places. When we say it together, it's like giving a cheer for Jesus and the rest of our team.

Listen to the Apostles' Creed and say it aloud until you have memorized it. If someone asks you, "What do you believe?" these words will help you to say exactly what that is.

I believe in God, the Father Almighty, the Creator of heaven and earth.
And in Jesus Christ, His only Son, our Lord:
Who was conceived by the Holy Spirit, born of the Virgin Mary,
Suffered under Pontius Pilate, was crucified, died, and was buried.
He descended into hell.

The third day he rose again from the dead.
He ascended into heaven and sits at the right hand of the
*   Father, Almighty.*
From there He shall come to judge the living and the dead.
I believe in the Holy Spirit, the holy Christian church, the
*   communion of saints,*
The forgiveness of sins, the resurrection of the body,
And the life everlasting. Amen.

The Best Call You Can Make

One of the best things about having God's Son, Jesus, as your friend is that you can tell Him everything, whether it's good or bad, and He will always listen to you. He loves you and always has time for you.

Talking with God through His Son is called prayer. You can pray anytime and anywhere, out loud or silently in your heart.

Jesus said that everyone who believes in Him is a child in God's family. There is one prayer that Jesus taught His friends to say. He wanted everyone in God's family to know how to get in touch with His heavenly Father anytime, day or night.

Do you remember when your dad or mom taught you your phone number? They told you to memorize it so you can call them whenever you need them or when you just want to talk to them.

One day Jesus' twelve disciples asked Him how they could call God, His Father in heaven. They wanted Him to teach them how to pray. Then God (their Father, too) would listen. Do you know what the words are? They're in a special prayer called the Lord's Prayer. Some people call it the "Our Father." It is a prayer that God's children have prayed together for hundreds of years. You can memorize it and say it whenever you like. You can say it whenever you are together with your church family.

The Lord's Prayer is a way for you to keep in touch with your heavenly Father. Once you learn this prayer, you'll know what kinds of things you can talk to God about. You can use the words in the prayer Jesus taught. And you can pray about the same kinds of things in your own words, too.

Listen to the Lord's Prayer and pretty soon you will be praying right along. You will be calling your Father in heaven and talking to Him with the words that God's Son, Jesus, told His friends to pray.

You won't need a telephone for this conversation. Let's go ahead and call our heavenly Father right now!

—◦◦◦—

Our Father, who art in heaven,
Hallowed be Thy name.
Thy kingdom come, Thy will be done,
On earth as it is in heaven.
Give us this day our daily bread,
And forgive us our sins,
As we forgive those who sin against us.
And lead us not into temptation,
But deliver us from evil,
For Thine is the kingdom, and the power,
And the glory, forever. Amen.

NOTES

Chapter One: The First Generation

1. Harsh, Joseph L., *Confederate Tide Rising: Robert E. Lee and the Making of Southern Strategy, 1861–1862* (Kent, OH: Kent State University Press, 1998).

Chapter Two: The Second Generation

1. Harsh, Joseph L., *Confederate Tide Rising: Robert E. Lee and the Making of Southern Strategy, 1861–1862* (Kent, OH: Kent State University Press, 1998).

Chapter Three: The Third Generation

1. Genesis 32: 22–31.
2. Judges 7.
3. Jonah 1, 2.
4. Chandler, E. Russell, *The Kennedy Explosion* (Elgin, IL: David C. Cook Publishing, 1972).
5. Constructed in 1976, Dobson Hall is home to MNU's graphic design courses, as well as the marketing and IT offices. This two-story building was originally named the American Heritage Building, but when the founding head of the art department, Rev. James Dobson, died of a heart attack that same year, the building was renamed in his honor. Dobson Hall contains an art studio, classrooms, and faculty and staff offices. Cit: MidAmerica Nazarene University, 2030 E. College Way, Olathe, KS 66062-1899. http://www.mnu.edu/component/content/article/272.html.

Chapter Four: The Fourth Generation

1. Fox News Channel: *Hannity & Colmes*, October 9, 2007. Dr. Dobson interview includes his well-known pro-life pledge in his responses to Sean Hannity. http://www.foxnews.com/story/2007/10/09/exclusive-dr-james-dobson-talks -with-sean-hannity/.
2. Tushnet, Mark. *The Supreme Court on Abortion: A Survey;* Abortion, Medicine, and the Law (Third Edition: 1986), 162.
3. National Right to Life, Abortion History Timeline (1959–1998). http://www .nrlc.org/archive/abortion/facts/abortiontimeline.html.
4. U.S. Historical Documents: Franklin D. Roosevelt's Infamy Speech, December 8, 1941. The University of Oklahoma College of Law, Norman, OK. http:// www.law.ou.edu/ushistory/infamy.shtml.
5. U. S. Supreme Court. *Roe v. Wade*, 410 U. S. 113 (1973). FindLaw|Cases and Codes. http://laws.findlaw.com/us/410/113.html.
6. Fr. Shenan Boquet. "Researcher: 1.72 Billion Abortions Worldwide Over Last 40 Years." LifeNews.com. (April 1, 2013) http://www.lifenews.com/2013/04/01/ researcher-1-72-billion-abortions-worldwide-over-last-40-years/.
7. Dana Milbank, "The Pro-life Movement Faces a Cold Reality," *The Washington Post* (January 22, 2014). http://www.washingtonpost.com/opinions/dana-milbank -the-pro-life-movement-faces-a-cold-reality/2014/01/22/0e414950-83b3-11e3 -9dd4-e7278db80d86_story.html.

Chapter Five: What It All Means

1. 1918 Influenza: The Mother of All Pandemics. Centers for Disease Control and Prevention. Volume 12, Number 1—January 2006. http://wwwnc.cdc.gov/ eid/article/12/1/05-0979_article.htm.
2. The "Black Sunday" Dust Storm of 14 April 1935. National Weather Service, Norman, OK 73072. http://www.srh.noaa.gov/oun/?n=events-19350414.
3. "Amazing Grace! (How Sweet the Sound)" by John Newton (1779). Hymnary .org. http://www.hymnary.org/text/amazing_grace_how_sweet_the_sound.
4. "Find Us Faithful." Copyright© 1987 Birdwing Music (ASCAP) Jonathan Mark Music (ASCAP) (adm. At CapitolCMGPublishing.com) All rights reserved. Used by permission.

Chapter Six: My Journey

1. Books by Danae Dobson. http://www.goodreads.com/author/list/29237. Danae _Dobson.
2. Ryan Dobson, *Wanting to Believe* (Nashville, TN: B&H Publishing Group, 2014).
3. H. Norman Wright, *In-Laws, Outlaws: Building Better Relationships* (Irvine, CA: Harvest House Publishers, 1977).

4. Michael D. Waggoner, "When the Court Took on Prayer and the Bible in Public Schools," *Religion & Politics* (June 25, 2012) http://religionandpolitics .org/2012/06/25/when-the-court-took-on-prayer-the-bible-and-public-schools/. See also: U. S. Supreme Court, *Abington School Dist. v. Schempp*, 374 U. S. 203 (1963). http://caselaw.lp.findlaw.com/scripts/getcase.pl?navby=CASE&court=US& vol=374&page=203. Cheryl K. Chumley, "Bible Ban: Wisconsin university system removes book (Gideon Bible) from campus center rooms," *The Washington Times* (January 16, 2014). http://www.washingtontimes.com/news/2014/jan/16/wis consin-university-system-bans-gideons-bibles-ca/?utm_source=RSS_Feed&utm _medium=RSS. David Barton, "America's Most Biblically-Hostile U. S. President," WallBuilders (2014). http://www.wallbuilders.com/libissuesarticles.asp?id=106938.

5. Dale Buss, *Family Man: The Biography of Dr. James Dobson* (Carol Stream, IL: Tyndale House Publishers, 2005), 66.

6. Ibid., 68.

Chapter Seven: Apologetics for Kids

1. 1 Samuel 2:12–17, 22–25, 30–34; 3: 11–14; 4: 12–21.

2. James C. Dobson, *Bringing Up Girls* (Carol Stream, IL: Tyndale House Publishers, 2010), 9.

3. George Barna, *Transforming Children Into Spiritual Champions* (Ventura, CA: Regal Books, 2003), 34.

Chapter Eight: Reaching Our Prodigals

1. Matthew 18:19 (KJV).

2. "Tough Love for Kids" (Parts 1, 2, 3), *Dr. James Dobson's Family Talk* daily radio program (March 3, 4, & 5, 2014). http://www.drjamesdobson.org/Broadcasts/ Broadcast?i=30166dab-93d3-43cf-a2ae-2cc698984a51.

3. "Neville Chamberlain Appeasement World War II," VideoWorldOnline.EU (2008). http://www.videoworldonline.eu/video/-CAAqfS8lUQ/neville-chamber lain-appeasement-world-war-ii.html#.U2nZLChjOBI. "Neville Chamberlain," Wikipedia http://en.wikipedia.org/wiki/Neville_Chamberlain.

4. James C. Dobson, *Love Must Be Tough* (Carol Stream, IL: Tyndale House Publishers, 2007).

5. Ibid. http://www.drjamesdobson.org/Broadcasts/Broadcast?i=30166dab-93d3-43 cf-a2ae-2cc698984a51.

6. The Pinery at the Hill, Colorado Springs, CO 80905. stephanie@thepinery .com Ph. 719-475-2600.

Chapter Nine: Reaching Our Unsaved Parents

1. Tom Brokaw, *The Greatest Generation* (Random House Publishers, 1998). http:// www.nytimes.com/books/first/b/brokaw-generation.html.

2. James C. Dobson, *Bringing Up Boys* (Carol Stream, IL: Tyndale House Publishers, 2001).

Chapter Ten: Words Matter

1. Josh McDowell, "Helping Your Kids to Say No," *Focus on the Family*, October 16, 1987.
2. Ibid., 217.
3. Greg Johnson and Mike Yorkey, *Daddy's Home* (Wheaton, IL: Tyndale House Publishers, 1992), 56.
4. Joyce Milton, *The First Partner* (William Morrow and Co. Inc., May 1999). Book reviewed by Cheryl Lavin, "Deconstructing Hillary," *Chicago Tribune*, April 25, 2000. http://articles.chicagotribune.com/2000-04-25/features/0004250032_1_hillary-clinton-pop-quiz-first-lady/2.

Chapter Eleven: The Saga of Two Good Men

1. College of Healthcare Information Management Executives (CHIME), Ann Arbor, MI 48104-4250. http://www.cio-chime.org/chime/boardandstaff.asp?
2. Champion Coach, Greenville, SC 29615. http://www.championcoach.com/MeetOurTeam.aspx.
3. "Bill Rogers (golfer)," Wikipedia. http://en.wikipedia.org/wiki/Bill_Rogers_(golfer).
4. "National Day of Prayer Task Force Men's Prayer Meeting," April 26, 2013. (FRC University Library.) http://www.frc.org/university/national-day-of-prayer-task-force-mens-prayer-meeting.
5. Ibid. http://www.frc.org/university/national-day-of-prayer-task-force-mens-prayer-meeting.

Chapter Thirteen: The Deeper Meaning of Legacy

1. John Sedgwick, *Rich Kids* (William Morrow & Co., 1985).
2. "People" (popular song), © 1963 & 1964; words: Bob Merrill; music: Jule Styne; publisher: Chappell & Co, Inc. (now Warner/Chappell Music).
3. "The Demonic Ape," *BBC Two*, Thursday 8 January 2004, Dr. Jane Goodall interview. http://www.bbc.co.uk/science/horizon/2004/demonicapetrans.shtml.
4. John Dalberg-Acton, 1st Baron Acton, *Letter to Bishop Mandell Creighton*, April 5, 1887. Published in *Historical Essays and Studies*, edited by J. N. Figgis & R. V. Laurence (London: Macmillan, 1907).
5. Florence Jones Hadley, "Are All The Children In?" Poetry @ The Lord's Rain. http://www.raindrop.org/rain/poets/chr17.shtml.

Appendices

1. Robert and Bobbie Wolgemuth, *How to Lead Your Child to Christ* (Carol Stream, IL: Tyndale House Publishers, 2005).

PHOTO CREDITS

Insert Page 6:   Jim caught in a pensive mood. (Credit: Harry Langdon)

Insert Page 6:   Jim and Shirley on their fiftieth wedding anniversary. (Credit: Greg Schneider)

Insert Page 10: Danae Dobson. (Credit: Greg Schneider)

Insert Page 11: Recent Dobson family portrait. (Credit: Harry Langdon)

Insert Page 11: "Jimpa" and "Mae Mae" with Lincoln. (Credit: Laura Dobson)

Insert Page 11: Granddaughter Luci. (Credit: Laura Dobson)

Insert Page 13: Shirley and Jim entering the East Room of the White House. (Credit: AP photo/Pablo Martinez Monsivais)

Insert Page 13: The Dobsons and President George W. Bush in prayer during National Day of Prayer event. (Credit: AP photo/Ron Edmonds)

Insert Page 14: The Dobsons with Pope John Paul II. (Credit: www.fotografiafelici.com, Rome, Italy)

Insert Page 15: Dr. Dobson during brief pre-Olympics run, 2002. (Credit: *Colorado Springs Gazette*/Carol Lawrence)

Insert Page 15: Dr. and Mrs. Dobson in Chicago at Radio Hall of Fame induction, 2008. (Credit: Donald Pointer Photography)

Insert Page 15: Jim and Shirley cut the cake. (Credit: Kevin Still)

Insert Page 16: Jim frying chicken. (Credit: Taken from *Welcome to Our Table*, by Shirley and Danae Dobson. Harvest House Publishers. Photo copyright 2012 by Julie Johnson, Vine Images. Used by permission.)

Insert Page 16: Shirley's Easter table. (Credit: Taken from *Welcome to Our Table*, by Shirley and Danae Dobson. Harvest House Publishers. Photo copyright 2012 by Julie Johnson, Vine Images. Used by permission.)

DR. JAMES
DOBSON BUILDING
A FAMILY LEGACY

WHAT WILL YOUR *Legacy* BE?

For decades, Dr. James Dobson's singular passion has been for the strengthening and preservation of the family. And now Dr. Dobson has created an eight-part film series to help a new generation of parents. Companion Bible studies have been written for each film, including *The Strong-Willed Child*, *Love for a Lifetime*, *Dare to Discipline*, and *Bringing Up Boys*, based on his books that have sold more than 40 million copies. *Member Books* include leader helps. *Leader Kits* include a *Member Book* and one interactive DVD with clips of Dr. Dobson and Ryan Dobson hosting and teaching. Want to finish well? Start building your legacy here.

DR. JAMES DOBSON BUILDING A FAMILY LEGACY

BUILDING A FAMILY LEGACY BOOKS

From Dr. James Dobson and Tyndale Momentum

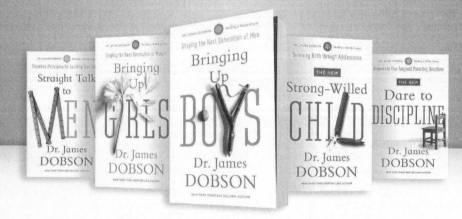

Bringing Up Boys • 978-1-4143-9133-5
Also available in hardcover (978-0-8423-5266-6) and audio CDs
(978-0-8423-2297-3)

Bringing Up Girls • 978-1-4143-9132-8
Also available in hardcover (978-1-4143-0127-3) and audio CDs
read by Dr. James Dobson (978-1-4143-3650-3)

The New Strong-Willed Child • 978-1-4143-9134-2
Also available in hardcover (978-0-8423-3622-2) and audio
CDs (978-0-8423-8799-6), as well as *The New Strong-Willed
Child Workbook* (978-1-4143-0382-6)

The New Dare to Discipline • 978-1-4143-9135-9

Straight Talk to Men • 978-1-4143-9131-1

AVAILABLE IN 2015

Love for a Lifetime
Revised and expanded edition
978-1-4964-0328-5

WHEN IT COMES TO LIFE, WE WANT TO GET IT RIGHT.

In *Wanting to Believe*, Ryan discloses the key messages imparted to him by his folks, sensible parents wanting to pass down truth to a stubborn son, covering topics like faith, finances, responsibility, identity, marriage, parenting, and the power of our words.

With irrepressible wit and wisdom, Ryan admits how he violated the hard-won lessons he'd been handed... and how he wound up loving them as his own in the end.

RYAN is the vice president of Broadcast at Dr. James Dobson's Family Talk, where he and his father co-host a daily radio show. Ryan lives in Colorado with his wife, two children, two dogs, and seven chickens.

AVAILABLE NOW IN PRINT AND DIGITAL EDITIONS

Every WORD Matters®
BHPublishingGroup.com